From Ghosts to Graduates

From Ghosts to Graduates is a timely book that recognizes that three years of interrupted learning has created an impending dropout timebomb of students who are traditionally at risk, as well as those who became disengaged during pandemic learning. Many students are ghosts in the system – they have become disconnected and disenchanted with schooling. Instead of only addressing strategies to treat the symptoms of dropping out, this important resource addresses the causes of the disengagement that led to those symptoms.

Author Emily Freeland shows how to identify existing and potential ghosts, how to reconnect students to the learning process and communicate that we see them and believe in them, how to overcome barriers to progress, and how to restore hope. Each chapter offers current research and practical strategies, as well as Do Now and Reflection sections to help you apply the ideas as you read.

With the deliberate practices in this book, you'll be able to change the trajectory of the ghosting trend and help more of your students be seen.

Emily Freeland has over 28 years of experience in education. She is currently serving districts and schools across the nation as an Instruction and Leadership Coach and is a certified National Dropout Prevention Specialist. Emily was awarded an Outstanding Curriculum Leader Award by the Alabama Association of Supervision and Curriculum Development. She was also a recipient of a Samford University Orlean Beeson School of Education Learning for Life Award.

D1478604

Also Available from Routledge Eye On Education
www.routledge.com/k-12

What Great Teachers Do Differently, Third Edition: Nineteen Things That Matter Most
Todd Whitaker

The Total Teacher: Understanding the Three Dimensions that Define Effective Educators
Danny Steele

Passionate Learners, Second Edition: How to Engage and Empower Your Students
Pernille Ripp

Working Hard, Working Happy: Cultivating a Culture of Effort and Joy in the Classroom
Rita Platt

Reinventing the Classroom Experience: Learning Anywhere, Anytime
Nancy Sulla

From Ghosts to Graduates

An Educator's Guide to Identifying and Reconnecting Disengaged Students

Emily Freeland

Routledge
Taylor & Francis Group
NEW YORK AND LONDON

Designed cover image: © Getty Images

First published 2023
by Routledge
605 Third Avenue, New York, NY 10158

and by Routledge
4 Park Square, Milton Park, Abingdon, Oxon, OX14 4RN

Routledge is an imprint of the Taylor & Francis Group, an informa business

© 2023 Emily Freeland

The right of Emily Freeland to be identified as author of this work has been asserted in accordance with sections 77 and 78 of the Copyright, Designs and Patents Act 1988.

Library of Congress Cataloging-in-Publication Data
Names: Freeland, Emily (Emily Seale), author.
Title: From ghosts to graduates: an educator's guide to identifying and reconnecting disengaged students / Emily Freeland.
Description: New York, NY: Routledge, 2023. |
Includes bibliographical references. | Identifiers: LCCN 2022033852 |
ISBN 9781032343747 (hardback) | ISBN 9781032341514 (paperback) |
ISBN 9781003321798 (ebook)
Subjects: LCSH: Motivation in education—United States. |
Underachievers—Education—United States. | Teacher-student relationships—United States. | Dropouts—Prevention—United States. |
Learning strategies—United States.
Classification: LCC LB1065 .F724 2023 |
DDC 370.15/4—dc23/eng/20220826
LC record available at https://lccn.loc.gov/2022033852

ISBN: 9781032343747 (hbk)
ISBN: 9781032341514 (pbk)
ISBN: 9781003321798 (ebk)

DOI: 10.4324/9781003321798

Typeset in Palatino
by codeMantra

This book is dedicated to all of the teachers who showed up for students during COVID and continue to show up each day. And to all of my road-warrior colleagues who go where they are needed.

Contents

Acknowledgements

When I started my doctoral research back in 2008, I had no idea how much that endeavor would change me as an educator. The voices of the students I interviewed are still with me even now. I could not have imagined the disappointments, barriers, and frustrations in their journeys through their schooling and to a high school diploma. But, I am glad I now know. Their stories have influenced the attitude I have each day I walk into a school building. Each one continues to remind me that, as educators, we have a tremendous power and influence over the dreams and future stories of our students. And, I am thankful to all of those who have played a role in helping me fulfill my dreams and write my future story.

There are some to whom I owe additional gratitude. Larry Headrick, my former boss and mentor, advocated for all students and taught me how to search for those who need us most, not only the ones in our schools, but also those in juvenile detention, youth homes, and alternative environments. My forever cheerleader, Lisa Beckham, epitomizes what it means to be a servant leader, and I am forever grateful for every door she placed in front of me. Kyra Donovan, who believes deeply in doing the right work, offered me the chance to step out of my comfort zone and take on a new adventure. Lisa Almeida, my friend and amazing leader, fostered the dream of completing this work and gave me the courage to take it on. Her continued support is allowing me an avenue to share it.

I am also forever grateful to those who helped to get this idea out of my head and onto paper. My colleague, Ann McCarty Perez, advised, suggested, and brainstormed on numerous Sunday mornings to help me clarify my thoughts and offer support. Doug Reeves not only helped me finish my dissertation all those years ago, but also provided guidance on how to start this process and a model for how to get it done. My dear friend, Melissa Dixon, read, re-read, corrected my grammatical errors, and gave insights that made each page better. And Lauren Davis, my editor, believed in my idea and made this endeavor a wonderful learning journey.

There is one who didn't want to be mentioned but has supported every degree and new job role, and makes me laugh every day. For moving things around the house when I'm gone, bursting forth with crazy songs and voices at odd times, hiding silly pictures in all of my stuff, and making my life a continuous adventure, I'm not mentioning you, Andrew.

Meet the Author

Dr. Emily Freeland has over 28 years of experience that includes administrative positions at the state, district, and school levels, as well as teaching science. She has supported school districts with the implementation of standards-aligned learning and rigorous instructional experiences. Much of her work has been concentrated in schools that were identified as underperforming and targeted the implementation of school turnaround principles, the effective use of data, closing achievement gaps, and increasing graduation rates. Emily has also served as a curriculum specialist and professional development director. In these roles, she worked with curriculum and assessment development, new teacher mentoring, at-risk programs, credit recovery, and instructional design. She has taught undergraduate and graduate courses in both science and education. Her work has included experiences in both traditional and online schools with developing effective instructional practices for all students. Emily is currently serving districts and schools across the nation as an Instruction and Leadership Coach.

Emily holds bachelor's and master's degrees in science education. She also holds an educational specialist degree, a doctorate in educational leadership, and is a certified National Dropout Prevention Specialist. Emily was awarded an Outstanding Curriculum Leader Award by the Alabama Association of Supervision and Curriculum Development. She was also a recipient of a Samford University Orlean Beeson School of Education Learning for Life Award.

Emily lives in Hoover, Alabama with her husband, Andrew, and her cat, Little Man.

Introduction

We Have a Ghost Problem in Our Schools

In my role as an instruction and leadership coach, I spend a significant amount of time visiting and working in classrooms. Sometimes school administrators come along with me, and sometimes I go to classrooms unaccompanied. One particular visit forever changed how I survey a classroom when I walk through the door. It was on a sunny fall afternoon that I began to see my surroundings differently.

On this particular day, I entered an eighth-grade science room where the energy was pushing the edge of chaos. The teacher was in a race to ask as many review questions as possible before time ran out. I watched the students wiggling in their seats as they threw their hands in the air to be called on to answer. One dark-haired girl, for some reason, caught my attention. She was dressed very plainly in a long, full, floral skirt, and faded blue t-shirt. Her hair was long, wavy, and a bit unkempt, and the frames of the glasses she wore were black, heavy squares that were a bit too big for her face. Initially, she was so enthusiastic as she waved her hand, hoping to capture the teacher's attention. But each time the teacher passed her over, the enthusiasm she had slowly waned. Her waving hand became lower and lower until she just sat quietly with her hands in her lap. Her excited smile and desire to share turned into what I could only interpret as a defeated disappointment. Right before my eyes, she faded into the background. She slumped in her chair with her eyes aimed at the floor. It was as though she no longer wanted to be there or to be seen. It was as if she became a ghost.

DOI: 10.4324/9781003321798-1

It was this encounter that made me think back on other times I had witnessed similar events. As I chronicled each memory in which I had seen students try to disappear, go unnoticed, or flee the classroom, my reflections led me to the realization that *we have a ghost problem in our schools*. Lost spirits are wandering our hallways and hiding in our restrooms. But most ghosts simply exist in our classrooms. Some of the ghosts are not easily seen, even though they are desperately trying to get our attention. They may be waving their hands to be recognized or staying around after the end of class to chat, but we fail to pick up on these ghosting signals they are sending to get our attention. Our ability to "see" those students who constantly ask questions and seek our attention and affirmation sometimes starts to diminish over time. Maybe it is the haste of the school day that causes us to miss seeing them or maybe it is the number who are seeking us. The subtle ways some reach out make them hard to detect.

Some spirits make sure we cannot help but see and acknowledge them in some way, positively or negatively. Those spirits enter our classrooms with an energy that moves desks, pushes other students out of the way, and causes papers to fly up in the air. You know, like a poltergeist. They are frequently frustrated and angry ghosts. Angry that they are there. Angry at their circumstances, and angry with everyone they know and encounter.

But then others are a bit harder to recognize. We usually find them toward the back of the classroom, and they often have their heads on their desks. A friend of mine describes these particular spirits as suffering from the four downs. They have their *heads down*, their *hands down*, they may be wearing *hand-me-downs*, and their outlook on life is *down-trodden* (Roller, 2018).

They come through the school doors day after day, week after week, year after year. Hoping. Hanging on to see if maybe today will be different. Maybe today will be the day someone sees them. Maybe today someone will care enough to reach out.

In your mind…look in your school, gaze down your hallways, and survey the back of your classroom. Do you see them? Do you see their faces? Do you know their names? Have you heard their stories?

An Exacerbated Problem

Most ghosts start out as eager students who want to feel a sense of belonging and who have a curiosity to learn. But as students progress upward in grade levels, finding the place where they fit in both socially and emotionally can be hard. Moving from spending the school day in one classroom with one teacher and a small number of classmates to a school day spent in multiple classrooms with different teachers with varying expectations and different configurations of a large number of students can cause anxiety and discomfort. Juggling all of this can cause students to withdraw because they do not feel safe where they are or confident in what they are doing.

In the report *Inequality at the Starting Gate* (2002), the authors share that as students enter kindergarten, there is a significant disparity in cognitive skills and abilities of disadvantaged students as compared to their advantaged counterparts. Many children, especially from homes of poverty, enter kindergarten with language deficits and an inability to control certain emotions or self-regulate behaviors. And, when students do not have the words to tell us how they feel, they can show us in really unappealing ways. Over time teachers can be heard saying things like "He's just so lazy"; "She's one of the low kids"; "That has to be the most unmotivated child I've ever had in my room"; or "Thank goodness her head is down. At least now we can have class, and she's not bothering anyone else." Does any of that sound familiar? I know I am guilty of both thinking and saying these exact phrases. What about "If he would even meet me halfway, I could help him. If *he* would only try?"

Maybe it is time to consider that these students are asking for help or a connection in the only ways they know how. What if they have lost all hope and wonder if it is even worth the effort to keep reaching out? What if they have failed so many times that they just believe that failure is inevitable? What if they no longer want to be seen? In *Achieving Equity and Excellence* (Reeves, 2020), we are reminded that it is the specific practices that teachers employ in the classroom that make the difference, not programs. It is time, then, for us to search for and utilize the best strategies to connect with and restore hope to those students who need us most.

As schools have emerged from the COVID-19 pandemic and returned to in-person learning from remote learning, it has become more and more apparent that the ghost problem has been exacerbated. With the number of students who "ghosted" during remote learning by never showing up or only existing as a non-communicative dot on the screen, we are not close to even scratching the surface of the long-term impact. Then there are the unintended messages we relayed during that time that caused students to question the length of the traditional school day and the importance of a connection to their teachers and peers. The impact of those messages has only begun to emerge.

Moving Forward

Ghosts have existed in our schools for a long time, and if we continue doing what we have always done, this will not change. It will only get worse. Why does it matter? It matters because ghosting is the path to dropping out, and it doesn't just suddenly start when students enter high school. We must take steps with intention to identify those students who are in the process of disengaging during the early years of their educational careers. If we focus on deliberate practices that are proven to re-engage students in the learning process and that have a high impact on improving learning experiences, we can change the trajectory of the ghosting trend.

In the chapters that follow, we will explore how we can identify existing and potential ghosts, review strategies that are most effective in reducing the ghost population, and examine practices to keep ghosts from disappearing altogether by physically leaving the building. In Part 1, we will begin our ghost hunt by looking at criteria that lead to disengagement and signal the ghosting process has started. In Part 2, we will explore ghost-whispering by examining strategies that reconnect students to the learning process and communicate that we see them and care, that their learning is important to us, and most importantly, that we believe in them. Finally, Part 3 will include opportunities for the practical application of strategies and steps to strengthen our teams, restore hope, and examine school and district policies that pose potential barriers to progress. Each chapter includes a "Do Now" task to provide opportunities for taking immediate actions. The "Do Now" tasks in Part 1 provide steps to identify your ghosts. Those tasks in Part 2 provide strategies to problem solve and find solutions to connect with the students you identified. The "Do Now" tasks in Part 3 identify larger factors that increase the potential for developing more ghosts. Opportunities for reflection will come at the end of each of the three parts.

Let's go ghost hunting!

Part 1

Ghost Hunting – How Do We Find Our Ghosts?

Hiding in Plain Sight

Ghosts have always existed in our schools, and we have recently experienced an uptick in sightings. When schools shifted to remote learning in March of 2020, none of us could have predicted that some schools and districts would not welcome students back to in-person learning again until August of 2021. Everyone who participates in K-12 education (students, teachers, administrators, and parents/guardians) struggled to navigate remote, hybrid, and in-person learning during the 2020–2021 school year. This was also the time that many students disappeared. According to an article published by *Education Week*, America lost more than 1.3 million students during the 2020–2021 school year (Pendharkar, 2021). These students disappeared from schools across the country. This loss spanned all demographics and grade levels, though the lower grades seem to be impacted more.

While many students never showed up on a school roster, others were only a black square on a screen. This was a constant challenge for teachers and administrators. It left so many questions as to whether the students were even on the other side of the screen, if they were doing the work, or if they were okay. I even spoke

DOI: 10.4324/9781003321798-2

with one teacher who said she would drop them off the call just to see if and when they would return.

The protocols used to keep students and staff safe and the way that remote learning was structured communicated some unintended messages to students that conflicted with how the school day was structured prior to pandemic learning. The effects of those messages are now surfacing. Some students are finding it hard to reconcile the importance of being back at school after remote learning. During remote learning, students had shortened school days and fewer requirements which were designed to lower stress and anxiety in the face of a really unique situation. But remote and hybrid schedules left many students without the structure and support they needed to be successful learners, so when they returned back to school on a full schedule, they were simply overwhelmed.

As teachers and administrators scrambled to provide alternative instructional opportunities and packets of activities, as well as to learn and to distribute new technology, we lost contact with many students, some of whom we had struggled to stay in contact with when they were in our buildings. When we emerged on the other side of pandemic learning, we found that things were more different than we could have predicted, and even more students had started to or had already become invisible.

As we anticipated the return to in-person learning, we threw around phrases like "learning loss" and "learning acceleration," while we planned for re-entry. What we discovered as we came together again was that large numbers of children not only missed out on the academic support provided during the school day, but they also missed the significant social growth that comes with personally interacting with their peers and teachers on a daily basis. We discovered that the learning losses were not nearly as significant as the loss of structure, preparedness, and connection that we all had prior to the closing of our buildings. These losses translated into students across all grade levels who no longer knew how to "be in school."

Elementary students missed out on years where they learn not only foundational skills for academics, but also the routines that lead to better achievement and behavior regulation.

The teaching of those routines starts in kindergarten. Due to COVID-19 protocols, those students who are in second grade as of the 2021–2022 school year did not complete a full year of kindergarten in a building and attended first grade remotely. The guidance students receive from their teachers in the middle years is critical to developing the maturity they need for high school and beyond, and that guidance was difficult to provide when students were learning remotely. The middle years provide experiences with different teachers for each subject area and managing to mix with other students while changing classes throughout the day.

For students in middle and high school grades, pandemic learning has translated into students who have unfinished learning and may be behind in credits. For those students who completed high school during this time, they face heading into the college and career world without having matured through the support of peers, teachers, counselors, and administrators. Additionally, three years of interrupted learning and the lack of structure and support is showing itself through more suspensions and expulsions across all grade levels but particularly in the lower grades, a trend we had seen diminishing with positive behavior interventions and restorative justice practices. We are now realizing the impact of emotional and physical trauma suffered by many of our students, too. Students who live in unsafe and unhealthy environments craved the refuge that schools provide, and teachers and counselors missed the indicators that signal the need for help.

Complicating Factors

In all of our schools, we have students who one of my colleagues refers to as "messy kids." Messy kids are those students who live a life that does not fit what we consider to be traditional or normal. Their life stories and family dynamics are rather complicated. They bring personal, social, and emotional baggage through the school doors every day that most of us could hardly comprehend. They take on roles outside of school that are those of an adult and should not have been theirs for many years to come. They are faced with making decisions that they are not equipped to make at such young ages. They look to us for help, support, guidance, and most of all, HOPE. We have discovered that pandemic learning has only served to create more of those messy kids due to the economic and health factors that impacted homes and families while many businesses and services were closed. And, as we have been back in our buildings, it has become increasingly clear that those kids are having a hard time reconnecting.

Knowing what we now know about the impacts of pandemic learning and the journey of students before the pandemic, each day that we fail to connect with those students who need us most, their hope and their spirits fade. Some of these students are easy to identify. Others are much harder to recognize. All of them now exist in our hallways and in our classrooms. It is, however, up to us to reach out and not only find ways to reconnect, but also to find ways to provide the support they need to move forward in their academic and personal journeys. It is time for us to go on a purposeful, targeted search for the ghosts in our schools.

1

Ghost Origins – Why Do Students Become Ghosts?

A Journey, Not an Event

Students disengage from the educational process for many reasons, and most of those reasons are related to academic, social, and emotional experiences. Those who disengage include all genders, races, achievement levels, and socioeconomic groups. We also know that students who, for whatever reason, are not engaged with school tend to be the ones who ultimately become dropouts. Even though it is more often characterized and addressed as an event, dropping out of school is a process that starts long before a student reaches dropout age. Those students with high absenteeism, chronic discipline issues, and failing grades have most frequently been on dropout lists and are identified with the highest ghosting probability. Interestingly, data has shown that students who dropped out of school missed an average of 16 days in the first grade as compared to only ten missed days for their peers who graduated (Alexander et al., 1997). For each additional absence, the probability of dropping out increased by 5%. Pause and think about that. Ghosting has already started in the first grade for some students.

DOI: 10.4324/9781003321798-3

Many of the causes of student disengagement that continue to plague schools were identified in *The Silent Epidemic* (Bridgeland et al., 2006). This report examined the perspectives of high school dropouts, probed the reasons students dropped out, and identified factors that would have encouraged them to stay in school. Although there are usually multiple reasons as to why students decide to leave school, the top five reasons that were stated included that classes were not interesting; they were behind in their coursework for missing too many days of school; they were influenced by others who had no interest in school; they had too much freedom and too few rules; and they were failing academically. It is important to remember that these factors do not just become an issue to students when they get to high school. Their influence is noticeable in the elementary grades and more evident in middle grades.

The return from remote learning has highlighted these same reasons that were stated, and the protocols established to address pandemic factors once students were back in our buildings only served to make these reasons worse. The national non-profit Youth Truth surveys students across the United States concerning their school experiences each year, and the organization continued to gather data during pandemic learning. The results from surveys in the Spring and Fall of 2020 and Spring of 2021 compared findings both pre-COVID shutdown and during COVID shutdown. Students reported that while in remote learning, only 37% found their classes interesting. The level of interest indicated declined as grade levels increased. This overall self-reported data was sharply lower than was reported pre-pandemic with 57% saying they learned a lot each day versus 39% during the pandemic ("Students Weigh In, Part III", 2021). This information suggests even more student disengagement for remote learning as compared to in-person learning.

Student and teacher absenteeism presented incredible challenges and reached new highs post-pandemic. The return to in-person learning necessitated new health and safety protocols, which included mandatory quarantines for those who were sick as well as close contacts. As a result, chronic absenteeism dramatically increased. Multiple school districts across the country saw attendance rates drop below 70% (Calvert & Chapman, 2022). Not only does absenteeism impact academic progress, but it also slows social maturation. Students fell behind from missing instruction and peer contact. Many districts also did away with hybrid learning options once buildings reopened. So, students in quarantine multiple times lost the opportunity to connect with their classes for real-time learning and to keep from becoming even further behind.

Outside But Inside

The impact of out-of-school or home factors can be as great as the impact of in-school factors. We often forget or even ignore that we have students in our rooms who are hungry and tired, anxious, scared, and frustrated. They may have listened to their parents fight or heard gunfire ring out in their neighborhoods throughout the night. They may not have eaten since they had their school lunch the previous day. They may have had to care for younger siblings because their parents work a night shift, or maybe they have to work a job themselves to help support the family. When it comes to these types of life experiences, we often make an association of these scenarios with lower socioeconomic homes. But it is important to remember that affluent homes can also have similar dysfunctions. The closure of our buildings left students isolated from an environment more safe than home and where there were multiple distractions that impeded their learning. With shortened school days and no access to after-school programs or extra-curricular activities, many students had more free time and freedom, less structure, and fewer rules while at home.

When some students are dealing with significantly distracting home factors, it becomes almost impossible to be fully engaged in school. We were able to see and hear examples of those distractions during remote learning. Some students have better coping strategies and are more equipped to function or hide their needs. Other students become more withdrawn and absent, both physically and mentally, from what is taking place in school. They may be overwhelmed by all of the responsibilities and requirements of home and school to the point that they develop paralysis of involvement.

Evidence from years of research shows that outside influences on students cause interruptions in schooling and have a negative impact on academic continuity and success. Schooling that was interrupted for reasons like pregnancy, needing employment, incarceration, or falling too far behind academically to graduate significantly increased the rate at which students dropped out (Hoye & Sturgis, 2005; Watson & Gemin, 2008). Because the COVID pandemic has resulted in three years of interrupted learning for most students, there is a possibility of an increased number of students dropping out.

Inequitable Access

Both the pandemic and remote learning placed a spotlight on the inequities students experience across the country, across schools, across districts, and across classrooms. It is these inequities that fostered an environment that put additional students at risk of disconnecting from school. When access to school required a virtual connection, we discovered far too many students lacked access to devices and to the Internet. According to Youth Truth data, 23% of students who responded to the survey had little or no internet access and 13% had no access to a computer or device ("Students Weigh In, Part III", 2021). The impact on Black and Latino students was greater than that of other demographic groups. This digital deficiency caused many schools to depend on "packet learning" until they could catch up with one-to-one technology.

Once students had devices, internet access became the urgent need. Students and families were creative in finding ways to get students connected with their teachers. One principal shared with me that she had students who would walk to the area McDonald's just to login to their classes. In some rural school districts, buses were enabled with Wi-Fi and deployed into remote areas so students had access to their teachers. We saw the divide between students who had devices versus the ones who did not and the learning curve associated with students just being able to connect with their teachers.

Some parents were able to support their children with their school work and keep them focused during the day, as many parents were able to work from home. Other parents had to be onsite for their jobs, which meant their children were unattended or in the care of older siblings or family members. The lack of support and structure during daily learning time served to widen the gap for students who already struggled to focus in the classroom.

Many educators equate dropping out with disappearing from the building. While there are students who do physically drop out and disappear, others drop out mentally and emotionally while remaining in our classrooms. Those who remain are the ghosts who are still waiting for a connection or who are compliant enough to go along so as to avoid confrontation or disruption. The more they disconnect, the more they fade, and the harder it is to re-establish a connection.

Do Now:

Consider your experiences with students before, during, and after remote learning.

1. How many of your students disappeared during remote learning?
2. Which students suffer from chronic absenteeism?
3. Which students have outside factors influencing their day in school?
4. Which students lack support at home?
5. How are these situations impacting learning and the ability to stay connected to school?

2

Ghost Indicators – How Do We Recognize When It Is Happening?

Old Problem, New Twist

In 2005, it was estimated that one-third of high school students in the United States left school without earning a diploma (Barton, 2005). To reduce high dropout rates, states, districts, and schools utilized multiple strategies and interventions to re-engage disengaged students and help recapture credits for those students with credit deficits. As a result, dropout rates declined to their lowest in history leading up to March 2020 (Barnum, 2022). This was partly due to stricter monitoring of graduation rates which was a component of the accountability measures under the 2001 *No Child Left Behind* (NCLB) legislation. NCLB used graduation rates as an indicator for how well students were being educated. It required graduation rates to be reported at the state, district, and school levels. This prompted schools and districts to look more closely at the students who were counted as graduates and as dropouts.

As we moved forward with the NCLB accountability measures, cleaned up the data, and did a better job of tracking student transfers and course completion, graduation rates rose dramatically and quickly. Credit recovery programs and continuation

DOI: 10.4324/9781003321798-4

schools were established, and there were more opportunities for students to recover lost credit, address grade deficiencies, and get back on track for graduation. In some cases, those students who were once closely monitored were shifted somewhere else so they no longer impacted the accountability at the traditional home school, and the students most likely to drop out were localized to a special site (Freeland, 2013). This shift caused rises in graduation rates that did not necessarily represent more students actually graduating. With the rates of students earning a high school diploma holding steady above 80% through 2019, dropout rates lost their place on the "hot topic" list. Even though we still lost some students each year, the problem seemed manageable. Our focus was on early intervention.

The impact of the last three years has left us all changed in some way. Almost everyone knows someone who lost employment and means of support, who lost loved ones, or who lost connections to friends and family. Our students suffered these losses, too, and many of the students who walked out of our classrooms in March of 2020 when schools across the country were mandated to close returned to us as different people. The experience of remote and hybrid learning changed how students access learning opportunities and also impacted the rate at which they were able to learn. These losses and different learning experiences have translated into more students who are frustrated and struggling to find their way academically, socially, and behaviorally.

As students are acclimating back to in-person learning, teachers are feeling the pressure to get them caught up on missed concepts as state testing deadlines loom and are, therefore, resorting to traditional practices like lecture and direct instruction to speed through as much content as possible. Students are increasingly withdrawing because of feeling overwhelmed with the assigned workload, and they are bored and see no value or relevance for their learning ("Students Weigh In, Part III", 2021). While we feel like it is a "now" problem, this is going to create long-term problems that will serve to undo all of the progress schools have made to decrease dropout rates and, therefore, has created for us a ticking dropout timebomb.

After school buildings closed in the spring of 2020 and for the 2020–2021 school year, graduation requirements were waived in some states to keep from penalizing students for issues and challenges created by the emergency learning situation into which they were thrust. Because requirements were lowered, some states actually saw increases in graduation rates for the 2019–2020 school year. Preliminary data for the 2020–2021 school year, however, is showing the opposite. At least 20 states have reported declines in graduation rates. Some of the factors attributing to the unexpected decline are that students were taking on more hours at a job, while others reported having to care for younger siblings (Barnum et al., 2022). More students reported being tired and feeling unmotivated due to a lack of connection to their teacher and peers. With graduation rates always being published in arrears, we likely will not know the real impact of pandemic learning on dropout rates until 2023 and beyond.

Those at Risk

Considerable research has been conducted to determine the at-risk factors contributing to students' decisions to drop out of high school. In *The Silent Epidemic*, the authors state, "The dropout epidemic in the United States disproportionately affects young people who are low-income, minority, urban, single-parent, children attending large, public high schools in the inner city" (Bridgeland et al., 2006, p. 1). Additional at-risk factors that have been identified include being male, having multiple siblings, having a younger mother, and living in a single-parent home (Alexander et al., 1997). Other typical indicators are parental attitudes, disruptive family dynamics, changing schools in the first grade, and being over age for a grade level (Dalton et al., 2009).

The fallout from pandemic learning, however, requires that we look differently at the criteria for who is considered at risk of dropping out and how their needs might best be served. The three key factors that have been used to determine dropout risk – chronic absenteeism, course failures, and discipline issues – now plague more students as remote learning and pandemic protocols created learning barriers for students and caused these factors to have an increased impact (Hollingsworth, 2021). Quarantine protocols and inequitable access to devices and the internet facilitated more students meeting the criteria for chronic absences and course failures. New students meeting these criteria may need different interventions from those students who were identified prior to the pandemic, as some of the causes were due to quarantine guidelines and COVID protocols.

Addressing dropout risk is important because students who fail to graduate from high school impact many aspects of society. In *Fearless Schools* (2021), author Dr. Douglas Reeves states that in 30 years, those students we failed to properly support during the pandemic will be well into their adult years, and if we do nothing differently, they will suffer the impacts of poverty and the associated ill-fated effects. The ill effects for those without a high school diploma include being more likely to be unemployed, generally less healthy, and at a higher risk of potential incarceration (Amos, 2008). It should be noted that this is not a minor issue and impacts high percentages of young dropouts, as "most wander through life like lost travelers, without guidance or goals, and many end up in prisons" (Barton, 2005, p. 5).

Reexamine Grade-Level Retention

Those who follow Dr. John Hattie's *Visible Learning* research closely and are familiar with his ranking of effect sizes know that almost all practices educators implement to help students have a positive impact on achievement (Hattie, 2017). There are just some that are more positive than others. There are also very few factors that have an actual negative impact on students. Grade-level retention is one of those with negative impacts. Retention reduces engagement and motivation in later grades and increases the probability of a student dropping out of school (Roderick & Nagaoka, 2005). Students who are retained generally have no sustained academic growth in learning beyond the year they were retained and are more likely to perform poorly in subsequent grades (Allensworth & Easton, 2007; Hwang & Capella, 2018). There is also evidence that being retained one grade in elementary school doubles the chances a student will drop out in middle school, and being held back in school is the most significant factor in predicting which students will drop out of school before the age of 17 (Goldschmidt & Wang, 1999; Hughes et al., 2018).

The criteria for retention almost always include poor academic performance and excessive absences. When students have academic struggles in early grades, there is an increased risk of lower academic achievement as they move ahead (Garnier et.al, 1997; Hwang & Capella, 2018). Students who dropped out of school performed at lower levels than their classmates in core academic courses as early as kindergarten (Hickman, et al., 2008). Subsequently, students who repeat multiple grades are three times more at risk of dropping out than students who have not been retained. Additionally, students who are retained once between kindergarten and sixth grade are at least two times more probable to drop out than students who are promoted (Hughes et al., 2018; Roderick, 1994).

Evidence also indicates that the grades during which retention occurs impact the rate at which students drop out. Being retained between kindergarten and third grade is associated with a 75% increase in dropout risk. Retention between fourth and sixth grade increases the dropout risk to 90%. At least 29 states have instituted retention laws for third-grade students who are not reading on grade level as measured by standardized tests (Wright, 2021). Some of those laws were enacted during the pandemic as a result of the anticipated impact of unfinished learning.

Grade retention also means that a student is now older than their grade-level peers, and approximately half of the students who are over-age for their grade drop out (Roderick, 1994). If a student is retained in more than one grade level, it creates a situation where the student will "age out" before they can "get out." Retention as a form of intervention does not address the academic needs of at-risk students or prevent them from dropping out of high school (Davis, 2021; Jimerson et al., 2002).

To mitigate the number of students at risk of retention, relaxed promotion procedures were instituted during pandemic learning. Data shows that the number of students failing at least one course has increased dramatically as remote intervention structures failed to meet the needs of most students who were facing academic challenges (Gross, 2021). The impact of these changes will be evidenced in the coming years. Interestingly, during this same time in the pandemic, there was an increase in the number of parents who were requesting that their children have the opportunity to repeat their current grade level. Some parents understood that their children had abbreviated access to learning, and they wanted their children to be able to complete what may have been missed (Davis, 2021). This request for retention came even as students performed satisfactorily on the work that they were assigned. The practice of retaining students who have successfully completed a grade has been highly discouraged over the years, as this can create all of the issues related to being older than grade-level peers.

The Critical Years

Ninth grade has long been a critical year for determining high school success, and as of the 2021–2022 school year, there are ninth graders whose learning was interrupted the second half of their seventh-grade year and continued into a third year of interruption due to quarantining guidelines. We might also be reminded that students who were eleventh graders in the 2021–2022 school year were expected to meet grade-level standards with only a partially uninterrupted ninth-grade year, a tenth-grade year of remote learning, and having missed the full experience and learning of the foundational years of high school. Significant evidence has been collected to show that successful transition from middle school to high school is a determining factor in students' decisions to stay in school, and success in ninth-grade courses sets the path for high school completion.

As further support for a successful ninth-grade transition, a study conducted in Chicago public schools revealed that students who had accrued the number of credits needed to be promoted from ninth grade to tenth grade were three and a half times more likely to graduate on time in four years than students who lacked enough credits for promotion (Allensworth & Easton, 2005). The study also found that course failures served as a good indicator for predicting whether ninth-grade students would graduate from high school. The graduation rate for ninth-grade students who received only one failing grade for a semester in a course, regardless of which course, was 20% lower than students who had passed all of their courses (Finn & Owings, 2006).

Data from a five-year dropout study of Philadelphia schools showed that approximately half of the students who dropped out in the school years from 2000 to 2005 were identified as at-risk in the eighth grade (Neild & Balfanz, 2006). This study indicated that 80% of the students who dropped out were either at-risk eighth graders or at-risk ninth graders. It also concluded that attendance rates of less than 70%, earning fewer than two credits, and being retained were identifying factors of ninth graders who dropped out. Students had a 75% chance of dropping out if they had just one of these characteristics in the ninth grade, even if they had not been identified as at-risk in the eighth grade.

Students who enter high school performing below their grade-level peers in math and reading are 50% more likely to fail one or more core courses than those students who are performing on grade level (Roderick & Camburn, 1999). Males are more prone than females to fail core courses with Hispanic males being most at risk of failure. Students who enter high school over age for their grade are more disposed to experience course failure. Two-thirds of ninth-grade students who experience failure in the first semester of the school year continue to experience academic difficulty in the second semester. Students fail courses for three reasons – they do not attend class; do not complete required work; and do not pass major exams (Roderick & Camburn, 1999).

The middle school years are critical for preparing students for success in high school. It is during this time that students begin to manage a new schedule, which includes changing classes and teachers throughout the day. It is also when the foundational skills of Algebra 1 are learned. Algebra 1 has long been the gateway course to math success in high school, as well as one of the main indicators for potential dropouts. Students also extend their reading stamina and strengthen the reading-writing connection while in the middle grades. The interruptions in learning have slowed this progression for many students resulting in time needed to shore up these skills. Additionally, the middle years are when students begin to figure out their interests and build their social networks. While many students typically struggle in these areas even under regular conditions, remote learning and the lack of available out-of-school community activities left those students socially disconnected and immature in many of their social behaviors.

Finding Solutions

The rising number of missing students due to the pandemic shutdown means this problem is only going to get worse. Even as school districts increase utilization of credit recovery programs, dropout programs, and continuation schools, shuffling students to different sites and programs might not necessarily give them access to the learning supports they need. For many students, school is the one constant in their lives, and, for a time, they lost access. The pandemic left us all changed in some way, and it left us with students who are different learners with different needs. Some of those needs are now interfering with their learning, making them a new risk group. As a result, it is imperative that our focus be on strategies and practices that mitigate new risk factors for ghosting and dropping out.

Do Now:

Examine the data of your students.

1. Which students are over-age in comparison to their grade-level peers?
2. Which ones have been retained and in which grade(s)?
3. Which of your students currently have credit or grade deficits?
4. Which students currently have failing grades?

Using the information included in this chapter, try to assess their risk of dropping out. What factors are they exhibiting?

3

Ghosting Beyond the Numbers – What Strategies Can We Utilize and What Steps Can We Take to Connect with Our Ghosts?

The Information Void

Personal connections between teachers and students were harder to establish in the virtual world and required different approaches because creating those connections had to happen through computer screens. This made it more difficult for teachers to get to know their students and develop a rapport that supports learning. The remote environment caused some students to feel anxious and uncomfortable, as many felt like everyone was staring at them when they were all on screen at once (Fisher, 2020). Being in-person for instruction allows teachers to get a much clearer read on students' moods, dispositions, and states of being during classroom time. Better decisions can be made about instructional adjustments or the types of questions to ask by using students' non-verbal feedback. Remote learning made it almost impossible for teachers to read students' faces

DOI: 10.4324/9781003321798-5

and body language or to pick up on non-verbal cues, especially when cameras were off. Even as teachers used more class time for social and emotional support strategies, they still lacked real-time information about students due to the disconnect of the remote environment. It was evident to both teachers and leaders that more informed decisions could be made about learning supports when students were physically in the classroom. As a result of this disconnect, academic, emotional, and mental health struggles went undetected.

With the return to classrooms, teachers are still seeing the barriers to learning that existed before the pandemic and are also seeing new barriers that are a result of the interruptions to learning students experienced during the shutdown. There are increased numbers of students having difficulty focusing, lacking self-regulation skills, and struggling with emotional control. Because the disconnect of remote learning left many teachers without the data and information needed to create the full story of each student, there are unknowns about their academic and personal needs. This means it is now imperative for us to pay closer attention to what our students are telling us subtly with their words and loudly with their actions. We have to ask "Why?" more frequently to get at the root causes of learning and behavior issues and to give our students more voice in their own learning. In this chapter, we will look at specific strategies to identify disconnected students and to give them their voice. Although the ideas that follow may already be familiar, the intention is to give these strategies new context and application for our current ghosts.

Good Intentions, Wrong Questions

While serving as assistant principal, one of my roles was to be the administrator representative on what was at the time called the Building-Based Student Support Team (BBSST). This team was composed of general and special education teachers, counselors, and an administrator and met bi-weekly to plan academic support for students who were experiencing academic challenges. Teachers submitted the names of those students of concern, and the team discussed possible interventions to support the students to be more successful. Sometimes the issues were related to discipline, and sometimes they were related to absences, but they were always related to grades.

One student in particular was discussed in every meeting. The submissions would come from different teachers, but the issues were always the same – he was frequently absent and had failing grades. He was a nice boy who was very respectful and not at all a behavioral problem. His standardized test scores indicated he exceeded expectations in each category, but he rarely turned in his assignments, so his grades were dismal. Maybe this student sounds familiar to you.

In each of our meetings, we tried to think of any intervention or support that might encourage him to complete his work. Finally, with the help of his family, we arranged for him to come to the office after school three days a week to catch up on his missing assignments. He dutifully arrived each time and worked diligently until it was time to go home. He would make progress but then have another string of absences, and we would start the cycle again.

After the first semester, his absences came to the attention of the district attendance officer. From the follow-up phone call regarding the next steps, we learned that during the previous school year, his mother had ended her life, and he was now living with his grandparents. The grandmother was disabled and did not drive, and the grandfather was still working and drove over an hour to his job. When the student chose to not get out of bed in the mornings, the grandfather was not able to spend the time to force the issue and would leave for the day. The grandfather shared that they rented a home in the community so the student could remain at his school for the rest of the year, as they hoped this would provide some stability. They needed our help because they, too, were worried about his academic and emotional health. They just had no idea where to go. We realized then we had been asking the wrong questions.

In schools, the processes and procedures used to analyze student needs often rely on quantitative data – grades, standardized test scores, numbers of absences or tardies, etc. While this data provides important information, it fails to tell the whole story of our students or the barriers outside of school that may have a negative impact on their academic success. The qualitative or anecdotal data from classroom interactions and observations, as well as conversations with students, fill in the gaps to complete that story. Unfortunately, that data is frequently missing from our analysis because it is more time-consuming to collect and requires more inferences as to causes. Our sense of urgency to get support in place for students pushes us to move forward quickly. As a result, we often end up doing interventions "to" students instead of "with" them, which then means the interventions may not get to the real cause of the barriers to learning.

If we challenge ourselves to slow down, have different conversations, and look at the full story from all data, we might learn information that takes us in a different direction from the one dictated by the quantitative data alone. In collecting student data, we should remind ourselves to focus on getting the full story and asking all the necessary questions to capture it. These next sections will share strategies to help us do that.

By Name, By Need

To ensure we head down the appropriate path for helping students and do it in a timely way, it is imperative that we know each student by both name and need. Grouping students according to grades, scores received on a screening assessment, or by indicators on a checklist do not get to the specific needs of each individual. We have to account for any other factors like social or emotional challenges that accompany those academic challenges.

Think back to the list you began compiling on your ghost hunt. Use the chart below to match names with needs. Consider the indicators listed in each column as an aid to help you make necessary determinations. This list is certainly not exhaustive and should be used to generate ideas to facilitate digging deeper with the data on hand.

Academic-Related Indicators	Social- and Emotional-Related Indicators
Failing Grades ◆ Specific Learning Deficits ◆ Missing Assignments ◆ Low Quality Work Absences ◆ Due to Illness ◆ Due to Transportation Issues ◆ Due to Family Factors Discipline Referrals ◆ Lack of Emotional Control ◆ Defiance ◆ Inappropriate Behavior or Language	◆ Never Smiles or Laughs ◆ Sleeps in Class ◆ Exhibits Off-task Behaviors ◆ Sits Alone in Class or Lunch ◆ Frequently Requests to Leave Class ◆ Negative Body Language

Also, consider visiting the classroom of a colleague who has many of your same students. Observe the behaviors and interactions of your students in a different environment. What do you notice and wonder? Consider that we sometimes fail to notice behaviors because we ourselves are immersed in the lesson. Simply observing students and their interactions can help to create their story.

Photo Quest
Ascertaining non-academic information about our students will provide insight to diagnose what may be causing a barrier to learning. This type of information can also help us know what connections a student has to others within the classroom and school. Data recorded may be extra-curricular memberships, club or organizational affiliations, employment, and interests

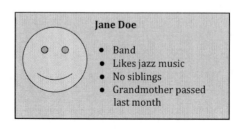

both in and out of school. Students without connections tend to have a higher ghosting potential. If you are unable to list information about a student, it is time to get to know that student a little better.

Create a photo chart that matches your seating chart. Include space for anecdotal notes about each student. Make sure to include at least three pieces of non-academic data for each student.

Listen to Hear

Schools should be a physical, emotional, and mental safe space for students and, if we are doing things right, a place where they want to be. Our students need opportunities to share their needs and how they think we can help. One way for us to give the students a voice in how we provide for their learning needs is simply to ask them. Consider the following sentence frames as a model and an opportunity to learn more about the students you serve. They can be used at any point during the school year as students' needs may change frequently due to changing circumstances in their lives.

For me to be excited to come to school and feel supported in class each day, I need…

A teacher who_____.
Classroom learning and tasks that_____.
An environment that_____.
Peers who_____.
Opportunities to_____.

This Is My Story

During a recent on-site support meeting with a district, the assistant superintendent invited us all to view a display that was composed of student works of art. The assigned theme for all was "My Story," and each piece was to incorporate multimedia techniques. Each art teacher serving in grades eight through 12 selected works from their students to submit. Viewing each of the works hanging on the wall was a very emotional experience. Each submission was an incredible show of talent, and while they were all amazing in their own way, some were both haunting and disturbing. On display were the voices of students telling us they were overwhelmed, sad or depressed, scared, bullied, and traumatized. Others displayed hope and gratitude. They each evoked an emotion and a connection to the artist. One that impacted me most showed a student wearing a mask that was smiling, and the other masks around the perimeter were sad, sleepy, and angry. It was titled "Help Me." At that moment, I thought about all I had seen and could only think, *What are our students trying to tell us that we haven't heard? What can we do to ensure their voices are heard?*

Think about the ways your students can share their stories. Maybe it is through journaling, artwork, or music, or maybe through a photo collage. Maybe they get choices for how they tell it. Whatever you choose, find a way to hear their story and provide continued opportunities for them to be heard.

Do Now:

Know Their Story

1. What additional steps can you take to know your students by name and by need?
2. What might they be trying to tell us through their actions?
3. How will you more intentionally ask "Why?" to get to the reasons for those actions?

Part 1 Key Points and Reflection Journal

Key Points

- ◆ Ghosts have always existed in our schools, but remote learning during the pandemic shutdown has increased the number of sightings as 1.3 million students disappeared in the 2020–2021 school year.
- ◆ Students disengage from the educational process for many reasons, and fallout from pandemic learning requires that we look differently at the criteria for determining who is at risk.
- ◆ Disengagement starts in the classroom, and we have to address the causes, not just the symptoms.
- ◆ One of the most important things we can do is find a way to hear the story of our students and know them by name and by need.

Reflection:

One idea that was new or presented a different perspective
…
I now think differently about…
For the next steps I will try…
I want to learn more about…

Part 2

Ghost Whispering – How Do We See and Connect with Our Ghosts?

Telling Ghost Stories

In a now-canceled television series, actress Jennifer Love Hewitt played the role of Melinda Gordon, a young woman who had the unique ability to both see and communicate with ghosts. Spirits, who still wandered among the living, would seek her help to pass on important messages and to get assistance in moving forward with their journey to the after-life. While the ghostly communications were sometimes confusing and presented challenges, Gordon knew it was important for her to figure out their needs and to assist as best she could. Because of this gift, she was called a ghost whisperer.

There are teachers who also share this special gift, and I have been fortunate enough to see them in action. One such teacher is Drew. Drew is as unassuming as a seven-foot-tall person can be, and I was in awe each time I visited his classroom. You see, his classroom is filled with ghosts. Drew's ghosts cross all demographic groups and ability levels while also including those who receive special education services, those academically below their grade-level peers, and those with behavioral challenges. Drew is an especially skillful whisperer because he watches for all signals that may come his way and does not wait for the ghosts to reach

DOI: 10.4324/9781003321798-6

out to him. He reaches out first. He recognizes that his ghosts often ask for help in very non-traditional and indirect ways, and he makes every effort to hear what they are trying to tell him. Drew sees and connects with each of them every day by standing at his door to greet them with a personal anecdote as they enter. He may ask about a family member, an evening activity, or their progress on a project, but his goal is to address them all individually. He constantly reassures his ghosts that he is there to help and support them. If he sees an academic or social-emotional need, he takes immediate action, even when his ghosts are too afraid or proud to ask. He does this because both their personal well-being and academic growth are important to him.

Drew continuously encourages his ghosts and also gently redirects them when they start to veer off track in their learning or behaviors. They know he believes in them. Most importantly, he is aware of each of their stories in great detail. Drew shared the stories of some of his ghosts with me. Some of those stories were sad, others were tragic, and some were even scary. Many of them have faced unimaginable hardships along their way that have left them withdrawn and untrusting. No matter, when the ghosts are with him, they are docile and engaged. Drew sees his ghosts and embraces their presence. He never rejects them. He understands and accepts the power of his gift. And, best of all, his ghosts know they can depend on his support. Ghost whisperers like Drew are an inspiration because they are relentless in their capacity to seek success for their ghosts. They do not just see their ghosts for what they are right now. They see them for what they have the potential to be.

In the chapters that follow, we examine strategies to support all educators with increasing their ghost whispering skills. Chapter 4 shares whispering strategies that communicate to our ghosts that they are seen, valued, and belong. Using these strategies helps build stronger connections to the teacher, school, and the classroom. Those connections are the first step. Chapter 5 offers ways to let our ghosts know that their learning is important to us. Creating engaging learning experiences that have value for life application outside of the classroom and allow students to see themselves in their learning fosters motivation and engagement. Finally, Chapter 6 provides strategies to instill confidence in our students that we believe in their ability to be successful both in and out of school. Removing self-doubt and fear of failure empowers our ghosts to know their possibilities are limitless.

Let's hone our skills!

4

Whispering in the Classroom – I See You!

Connecting for Learning

There are three quotes frequently cited whenever educators discuss the importance of relationships in schools. One from Dr. James Comer (1995), a noted child psychiatrist, states, "No significant learning happens without a significant relationship." The second quote has been attributed to many individuals, including Theodore Roosevelt, John Maxwell, and Earl Nightingale. It notes, "Children don't care how much you know until they know how much you care." The third comes from a 2013 TEDTalk given by renowned educator Dr. Rita Pierson entitled *Every Kid Need a Champion*. In her impassioned delivery, she says frankly that "Kids don't learn from people they don't like." These three quotes highlight the connection between relationships and learning. Strong relationships with and among students in the classroom create an environment that supports both social-emotional and academic learning ("Students Weigh In, Part III", 2021).

Intuitively, we know from experiences with our own teachers that these quotes make sense, as most of us have had encounters with teachers who either fostered our learning or created barriers

DOI: 10.4324/9781003321798-7

by making the learning environment uncomfortable (Bayram Özdemir & Özdemir, 2020). Dr. Comer (2020) elaborates that it is the positive connections students have with their teachers and with their peers that allow them to be accepting of the support needed to help them be successful. These positive connections create a psychologically safe environment in which students are not afraid to ask questions, take risks in attempting complex tasks, and gain the confidence to manage and direct their own learning and relationships. When they are confident and feel supported, students are able to learn the academic and life skills necessary to do well both in and out of school. Caring relationships with teachers also provide the encouragement students need to stay in school and reach graduation (Freeland, 2013).

Even though we may just feel or believe wholeheartedly that there is a strong connection between relationships and learning, evidence from research supports that this connection *does* indeed exist and is significant (Sethi & Scales, 2020). Consider the information below obtained from the Visible Learning MetaX website (www.visiblelearningmetax.com/Influences, accessed 5/4/2022).

Influence	Effect Size
Teacher Credibility (competence, trustworthiness, perceived caring)	1.09
Teacher-Student Relationships	0.47
Belonging (School Connectedness)	0.40
Teacher Subject Matter Knowledge	0.19
Students Feeling Disliked	-0.26

(Note: 0.4 effect size signifies an average year's growth in achievement for a year of learning. Anything above 0.4 is considered to accelerate learning.)

While each effect size has value in and of itself for understanding the impact of relationships on learning, they also support the intentions of the highlighted quotes when evaluated with respect to each other. The data confirms that the greatest impact teachers have on student learning comes when students believe their teachers care about them and their learning. Additionally, the data shows that students are not just more likely to accept support but are also more likely to seek help, accept feedback, and invest in the tasks teachers assign when positive student–teacher relationships exist (*Visible Learning – Home*, 2021). Further, relationships far outweigh the significance of teacher content knowledge alone. Of course, that does not mean just any person can walk in the school off the street and teach an Algebra class. An understanding of content and how it is best taught does matter and is most impactful when students are connected to their teachers and to their peers and also have a connection to the content they are expected to learn. Likewise, most students report wanting to perform better for teachers who they believe value and support them (Sethi & Scales, 2020).

By contrast, others have felt the negative impact on learning when they were not connected to the teacher or perceived the teacher did not like them. Perceptions filter and influence how students receive and process information, especially when those perceptions are negative. Negative perceptions of teachers have an adverse impact on how students view their learning opportunities and affect how students feel about themselves (Freeland, 2013). Negative perceptions often create an uncomfortable learning environment and foster feelings of anxiety and discomfort which, in turn, cause barriers to learning (Sethi & Scales, 2020). This further emphasizes the need to focus on positive interactions with and among students and to provide opportunities to establish strong connections. If we fail to address negative perceptions, we risk losing these students to ghosting, as they will remain disconnected from the classroom and from learning.

Connection Error

For students who struggled to connect with their teachers when they were face-to-face in classrooms, the divide created by remote learning made it even more difficult to build relationships. The communication lines were cut when school buildings closed in March of 2020, as large numbers of students had no access to the Internet or to devices ("Students Weigh In, Part III", 2021). Without a means to communicate with teachers, students found themselves isolated from the day-to-day routines of school and the relationships they had prior to school buildings closing. The shutdown left so many disconnected from their school friends, and it also kept them separated from community and club teams and church-affiliated activities. Their need to feel connected and have a place to belong had many students turning more to social media for those connections. As a result, students returned to school buildings with an over-reliance on virtual social media connections and without the skills needed to form good in-person relationships. This strong virtual connection and need to be seen was most evident as certain TikTok challenges became more organized and led to unfortunate behaviors and destruction throughout schools upon students' return, as these challenges required students to video their participation for others to view (Helmore, 2021).

Barriers created by shortened daily schedules, Internet connectivity issues, and limited availability of devices served to make it harder for students to access their teachers in real time. One assistant superintendent shared with me that her district had done a focus group discussion with some of their high school students. The students in this group shared that they felt isolated from their teachers and peers because remote learning made interactions harder. The sterile environment created by remote learning made it difficult for some students to engage with teachers and their peers. Many teachers and students were intimidated by breakout room options, so the smaller group settings needed to foster stronger relationships among students were not accessed (Tackie, 2022).

Both teachers and students felt the divide created by remote learning and the difficulty it created in establishing relationships. For teachers, those students who failed to sign on daily or who chose to keep cameras off made it impossible for connections to be made (Tackie, 2022). Teachers were unable to make virtual eye contact or pick up on non-verbal cues from students. Both of these types of interactions help to gauge the next steps for learning in the classroom, and they were nonexistent as cameras remained off. For teachers, this disconnect meant missing out on opportunities to identify, diagnose, and address student learning needs. For students, this meant missing out on the valuable learning connections that relationships with teachers and with peers provide (Ryzin, 2021). Now that schools are back with in-person learning, it is critical that teachers intentionally design opportunities to create stronger connections in the classroom (Gonzalez, 2015). The need for these connections is even more significant for students who were not fully connected before pandemic learning, as discussed in Part 1.

Know Them to See Them

One of the most anticipated events as summer ends and the preparation for the start of the school year begins is the release of classroom rosters. Both teachers and students are anxious to find out who will be in their classes and if they know someone else who is on the list. Open House times are scheduled for meet-the-teacher opportunities, and parents and students can be heard talking in the grocery store or at the ballfield about their new teachers and the excitement of being back in school. Making initial connections starts before students even enter the classroom for the first day.

As teachers arrange and decorate their classrooms for the arrival of students, name tents and seating charts are made so students have a designated place to go at the start. This often helps alleviate the anxiety created when students enter a new space and must decide where to sit or with whom to sit on the first day. Assigned seating indicates to students that they have a place in the classroom that is their very own and that they belong in this space (Wong et al., 2012). Seating charts provide teachers with a structure to get to know students' names more efficiently, and knowing students' names is an important step to learning who they are.

One way for teachers to show students that they are seen, known, and valued is by learning their names quickly at the beginning of the school year and by ensuring they pronounce them correctly (Cooper et al., 2017; Walker, 2021).

As classrooms become more diverse, teachers' willingness to create culturally, ethnically, and racially inclusive and respectful environments starts with appropriately acknowledging who is in their classroom. A person's name is a gift; it is one of the first things they are given in life, and as such is a part of their identity. When teachers mispronounce or shorten a student's name into a nickname without the student's request to do so, it can be interpreted as disrespectful and often leaves students demoralized. Incorrectly pronouncing a student's name is damaging to the student–teacher relationships because it is a sign that the teacher is not interested in extending the effort to truly know the student and, by extension, causes barriers to learning (Walker, 2021).

Each student comes to us with a unique identity and story. For students to feel connected to us and to their peers in the classroom, we must be intentional in the first days of school with how we learn the details of that identity and story. Their story begins as their names are shared with us. As they grow as individuals throughout the year and develop their interests and personalities, we must be committed to learning those details as each new chapter of their story is written.

Relationships Are Hard Work

When students returned to buildings after remote learning, one theme that was prevalent in the schools and districts I served was re-establishing relationships with students. During the first few weeks of the school year, while schedules are changed and classroom loads are balanced, teachers have traditionally invested time on establishing relationships with students. Plans are developed across multiple days to include activities for students to share about themselves and get to know each other, whether through name games or reflective writing prompts. These types of activities have always been common in the first days of school and provide a way for teachers to make connections through things each student shares. The disconnect caused by remote learning has now placed a priority on re-establishing the relationships that support learning (Trust & MDRC, 2021).

Relationships do not just organically materialize. They require hard work and intentionality. Maintaining good relationships requires investment. While time spent on relationships at the beginning of the year is crucial, time must be invested throughout the school year to strengthen classroom relationships. Integrating relationship-building strategies and skills into the context of daily classroom operations creates an inclusive classroom culture and communicates that all students are important. Turn-and-Talk, Think-Pair-Share, and Sentence Frames are all helpful, structured protocols that build speaking and listening skills and provide opportunities for all voices to be heard in the classroom. When student voice is an integral part of instruction, students feel a greater sense of belonging, are more engaged, and have higher academic success (Quaglia et al., 2020). As students' maturity and support levels change throughout the year, their relationship needs will also change. Consider trying the 2×10 relationship-building strategy that asks teachers to select a small number of students and purposefully engage in two-minute conversions with each one for ten consecutive days (Wlodkowski, 1983). These conversations can happen anytime throughout the school day. They just need to happen. A teacher recently shared she had tried this with a group of her students and mainly engaged with them on the walk to and from lunch. She was amazed at the things she learned about her students. She regretted not starting this strategy at the beginning of the year. The commitment to constantly work on classroom relationships takes time and effort, but when done well leads to better academic success and establishes an inclusive environment where all students are known, seen, and valued.

Interactions and Reactions

In a recent conversation with a colleague, she shared that her son was having a tough time with one of his teachers. As one of the compliant, "good" students in the class, he said his teacher frequently takes time to talk with him to see how he is doing and to connect on a personal level. She responded to him that it was good his teacher was making an effort to get to know him. What he said next she found both interesting and sad. He went on to say that he did not like this teacher and did not want her to make this effort to speak to him. He recounted disparities he perceived in her interactions with and reactions to other students. He felt she was inconsistent in her treatment of different students, and for that reason, he did not want to be connected to her. Actions and interactions in the classroom can sometimes invoke unanticipated reactions. When students see that others in the classroom are treated differently or inequitably, they can begin to disengage. As such, care must be taken to be consistent and fair with all students. Considering possible scenarios that might influence a bias, as well as how responses might be interpreted, will help to ensure students believe everyone in the classroom is valued equally and that student perceptions of those responses remain positive. Every interaction with a student should be approached as an opportunity to foster or break the relationship both with that student and with those who are watching.

It is our response in difficult situations that determines our relationship status with all students. When a student misbehaves or responds inappropriately, there is usually a reason, and it is incumbent upon us to find out the root cause. It is important to remember that for children who grow up or live in noisy, chaotic homes, that type of environment can become their normal. They find ways to be comfortable in that setting and understand how to navigate it. When they are at school where things are expected to be orderly and quiet, they are uncomfortable. Their response is to try to normalize their school environment to match that of their homes. When students are loud or speak out of turn, it usually is not out of disrespect or rudeness. To them, it is just normal. Instead of trying to label behavior, we should endeavor to understand it (Curran & the IRIS Center, 2003, 2021).

Additionally, we sometimes assume that students should know better. If students do not come to us exhibiting the behavior we expect, we should teach them alternatives. We can accomplish this by acting as the model. Showing the kindness and respect we want in return reinforces what we want from students and maintains relationships in the process.

When students exhibit undesirable behaviors, our first questions should be "Are you ok?" (Breaux, 2011) and "Why did you do what you did?" Starting here communicates that first, and foremost, you are concerned about them and care. Those are also two things students need to be able to verbalize so we can keep from breaking the relationship. It then provides the opportunity to discuss with the student what they might be able to do differently next time. These conversations with students must take place one-on-one and without the audience of their peers to help the student maintain their dignity. Taking this time to talk with students helps build a stronger relationship and provides the opportunity to teach the student a better way to handle the situation. This may not be the quickest way to stop the misbehavior, but it does help to maintain the relationship or to repair or re-establish the connection, if needed. If this last step is missing, the misbehavior is likely to reoccur because the relationship will remain broken.

It is often the reactions that break relationships, and discipline issues can be the cause or result of a broken relationship. Since students have returned from remote learning, suspension and expulsion rates have increased dramatically. While some have been warranted, others could have been avoided with different reactions that could have de-escalated events and behaviors. If we want different behaviors from students, we must teach the desired behaviors and self-regulation skills (Curran & the IRIS Center, 2003, 2021). Masterful ghost whisperers gauge their responses to de-escalate situations, when possible, then teach the desired behaviors. Most importantly, they build connections and maintain relationships, because that is critical to supporting student learning.

Do Now:

Create Your Plan

When thinking about the start of the school year,

1. What will you do to create a space where students feel they belong?
2. What strategies or activities will you use to learn students' names and correct pronunciations?
3. How will you continue to grow relationships throughout the year?
4. What steps will you take to *teach* and *model* desired behaviors?
5. How will you mend broken relationships as they occur?

Use these questions to guide the plan you develop to build and maintain relationships with students.

5

Fostering Engagement and Motivation – Your Learning Is Important to Me!

Attention or Engagement

Could I have your attention? This question is one that is heard often in classrooms, in conference rooms, and in ballrooms. It is used to get people quiet, to be still, to look at the speaker, and to focus. Most of the time, we all comply when that is asked of us. However, it is what happens in the moments that follow that determine if we stay that way. Think about the number of times you have been drawn into a lecture, keynote, or conversation based on the opening only to find your mind wandering minutes later. Our level of interest and engagement declines if we are unable to find ways to connect with the topic or the person delivering the message. If we see no inherent value to investing our time, we mentally move on and look for other things to do or to occupy our minds.

In a 2017 presentation, author Polly Patrick stated, "You can capture students' attention, but you have to invite their engagement." Think about how this applies to classrooms. This statement immediately resonated with me and caused me to reflect.

DOI: 10.4324/9781003321798-8

I thought about my early days of teaching and the times I had used a really cool science experiment to get students interested in what we were about to learn, but then moved on to my usual not-so-exciting lecture and problem-solving routines. I could do the attention part; it is pretty easy in a science class. It was inviting the engagement that I had not mastered. Not having made the distinction in my own mind between attention and engagement resulted in students getting excited about what they might get to do only to be let down by what I did instead.

How does attention differ from engagement? As it applies to learning, www.dictionary.com equates attention to careful observation but engagement to involvement. For students, that means the difference between being passive or active in the learning process. In *The Highly Engaged Classroom*, Marzano et al. (2011) move us through a series of questions that helps us consider the factors that impact our ability to capture attention or invite engagement. Deeper examination of these questions shows that engagement is a progression rather than something that is immediately attained. Those questions, delineated in the Table of Contents, are as follows: (1) How do I feel? (2) Am I interested? (3) Is this important? (4) Can I do this? The first question in the series, which addresses emotions, takes us back to Chapter 4 and the value of relationships, psychological safety, and connectedness in the classroom.

Even though students bring personal and emotional baggage through the school doors with them on any given day, a connected classroom environment can change a student's emotional state to be more positive (*The Power of Relationships in Schools*, 2019). If we are unable to address how students are feeling or to get them to an emotionally positive place, their minds will be unable to focus on anything else, which means we will not gain their attention. This fits with the often-repeated phrase of Maslow before Bloom emphasizing the need to meet social/emotional/physiological needs before trying to address learning needs. When we are purposeful at the start of the year with establishing a safe and connected classroom, we can more quickly transition to Marzano's next questions, as relationships provide the foundation. Those next three questions speak directly to how well we know our students, their interests and abilities, as well as how effectively we design instruction. If we choose to ignore the importance of these connections with our students, we risk the disengagement that causes ghosting.

In quickly scanning the classroom, it may seem easy to determine which students are engaged and which are disengaged. If there are students who have slumped down in their seats, have no books or papers on their desks, have bobbing heads as they fight to stay awake, or have their heads down and are asleep, then most of us would assume that they are disengaged. When students are facing the front with books open, nodding and making eye contact, or working diligently on the assigned task, we interpret those observations as engagement. Just because students may appear engaged does not mean that they are actually engaged. Many students are well-versed in how to play the game of school. They have mastered compliance. These students go through the motions and do as they are asked. They complete the tasks that are assigned and exhibit behaviors that meet the rules. Compliant students are good at the facade of engagement. Compliant students are focused on tasks completion and rule following; engaged students are committed to learning (Schlechty, 2011).

Inviting Engagement

In *Ask Don't Tell: Powerful Questioning in the Classroom*, Peery et al. (2013) write, "Questions are an invitation to learn and to connect" (p. 1). This was made very clear in an English Language Arts classroom I visited as the teacher was beginning class, and students were shifting their attention to the novel they had been studying. The teacher began by recounting the events from the chapter they had discussed the previous day. She chronicled the happenings, described the characters' development, and set the stage for what was coming up in the next chapter. I couldn't help but think that a huge chance to engage in conversation with the students had just been missed. As I looked around the room, I could see that some students had already mentally checked out and had slouched in their seats or were talking with each other.

They had already disengaged. Instead of taking the opportunity to use questions as a way to get the students to share what they remembered or how they connected with the story or characters, the teacher simply told them what she felt was important to remember. Her voice and perspective were what seemed to matter. In this situation, the invitation was never extended, and student engagement was not maximized.

In a typical class period, teachers ask many questions. That number has been estimated to be "between 300–400 questions per day and as many as 120 questions per hour" (Vogler, 2008, para. 1). That's a lot of questions! If you think this number seems too high, invite a colleague to sit in during one of your class periods and have them do nothing but record the questions you ask. All questions. You might be surprised by the results. Many of the questions that are typically asked are low-level, recall, or procedural (Vaish, 2013). If we want students to feel invited into the learning, we must intentionally plan questions that connect with them and spark their thinking. In other words, plan questions worth answering. It is also vital to allow students to think about how they will respond. Think time or wait time allows students the opportunity to process the question, formulate an answer, and also to contemplate the responses of others (Walsh & Sattes, 2015). Additionally, these pauses allow the teacher time to process the exchange and determine what follow-up or clarification is needed or where to take the conversation next. When teachers are too quick to move on to the next response or next question, they take away necessary processing time which then results in some students feeling left out. If teachers answer their questions themselves, students "don't get a chance to do their own thinking or take ownership…" (Asmus, 2017, para. 2). Additionally, "When you ask a question instead of giving the answer, the entire brain gets active as it reflects …" (Asmus, 2017, para. 7). Asking invites the whole brain to learn, which makes questioning a game-changer for engagement and learning in the classroom.

It seems reasonable to think that if "The one who does the work does the learning" (Doyle, 2011, p. 7), then the one who does the asking does the thinking. To further evoke student curiosity and deeper thinking, the task of asking questions should then shift to the students. Anyone who has encountered a small child has experienced the barrage of "why" questions that come with being curious about the big world around them. As educators, we also know that "why" questions hold high value for thinking, as it moves thinking to higher levels of Bloom's. If we want students to ask meaningful questions, we need to teach them how to create good questions. The Question Formulation Technique is a simple process that can be used to teach any person how to write better questions (*What Is the QFT?*, n.d.). Steps for generating questions move students from a topic of interest, through draft questions, to question analyst, all the way to their best questions. When students engage in generating their own questions, they become better thinkers, problem solvers, readers, writers, test takers, and life-long learners.

It's an Active Process

Questioning is a powerful tool to increase engagement, and it becomes even more powerful when it is used to facilitate classroom discussions. In examining the effect sizes from Hattie's MetaX website, questioning has an effect size of 0.48 and academic discussions have an effect size of 0.82 (Hattie, 2017). This means that when good questions are coupled with academic discussions, this combination has the potential to double learning. To maximize the impact of classroom discussions, they must be structured and planned. Planning should include both what we want students to accomplish and how they will do it.

But most students are not highly experienced with structured conversations. To set them up for success, discourse patterns should be taught and modeled so students can effectively share and challenge ideas. Talk Moves, facilitated discourse patterns, are an effective way to model how students can interact with each other through academic conversations. Structured protocols, like Sentence Starters, Think-Pair-Share, Socratic Seminar, Inside-Outside Circle, etc., promote equity in the classroom by providing opportunities for all students to participate and their voices to be heard. These types of conversations allow students to learn from each other and to build their own understanding through the shared ideas of others (Zwiers & Crawford, 2011). And, in case we need to be reminded, students much prefer talking to each other than talking to adults. By talking about their ideas and their understanding, students become better speakers and listeners, attain academic vocabulary and language, produce higher-quality writing and work samples, and form stronger connections to their peers.

In the article "The Engagement Illusion," Gupta and Reeves (2021) assert that "one of the greatest challenges teachers face in improving student engagement is correcting the perception that engagement is something within the student that cannot be influenced by the teacher" (p. 60). When teachers intentionally design lessons that include questions for deep thinking and employ a discussion protocol to maximize student voice and participation, engagement increases dramatically. If we leave engagement up to off-the-cuff questions and a general talk-among-yourselves attitude, we miss out on valuable opportunities to show students that their learning is what is most important to us.

Motivation for Learning

Both students and teachers have reported that student motivation is down since returning from remote instruction (Toth, 2021). The fatigue of Zoom classes still lingers, and it has taken students a long time to get back into all-day classes. Interestingly, engagement and motivation go hand-in-hand, which means when we increase student engagement, we also raise student motivation (Sousa, 2015). While on a coaching visit with a principal I serve, I asked him what he was hearing from students about their classroom experiences since returning from remote learning. He shared that more students than was typical before remote learning were reporting boredom. He relayed a conversation he had with one student who had been sent to the office for having his cell phone. This was of note because school policy requires all students to place their phones in a holding bag at the front of the room while they are in class. As the principal counseled the student through why having his phone was wrong and how it kept his attention away from his teacher, the student replied that he [the principal] was assuming that there was something worth listening to in the class. This is where we often make misjudgments about students' lack of motivation. Just because we love our content and find it interesting doesn't mean that students will (Gupta & Reeves, 2021). Further, motivation is not about what we as teachers do in the classroom, it is about what we get the students to do. Therefore, we have to design work for students that is worth doing.

Students value learning that is immediately useful to them, not something that they may need some years down the road or "gets them ready for college." Real-world, relevant learning for students is about their here and now. When learning has meaning for students and they can see how it can be applied in their own context, they are more motivated to persevere and complete assigned tasks. Students are also more motivated when choice is offered. Think of the ways that lessons could be related to the experiences of our students during the COVID-19 pandemic and remote learning. There are opportunities across all content areas to make connections. Whether looking at the biological characteristics of viruses, or the historical impact of past pandemics, or completing a statistical analysis of pandemic data, teachers could use a topic that is of significance to students at the moment to teach multiple academic standards. Students could be offered a choice for their area of focus, as well as a choice for how they will represent their learning be it through writing, an oral presentation, or an artistic representation. The community in which students live and the corresponding current events offer endless possibilities to make learning immediately useful. When students have choice in how they both learn and show their learning, they are willing to give more effort to the learning and produce higher-quality work (Marzano, 2011). When teachers know their students well and plan relevant and engaging learning experiences, students are motivated to do the work and stay connected to the classroom (Freeland, 2013).

Do Now:

Plan for Engagement
Think of an upcoming unit of instruction and the sequence of lessons you might use.

1. How will you purposefully plan for questions that invite students to connect and to learn? What questions will you ask to get students to think at higher levels?
2. What opportunities will students have to formulate and ask questions of their own?
3. How will students talk about and reflect on their learning?
4. How will you incorporate immediate application and choice?

6

Communicating High Academic Expectations – I Believe in You!

Unintended Messages

Noted writer Ralph Waldo Emerson is attributed as saying "your actions speak so loudly I cannot hear what you are saying." In the classroom, teachers both intentionally and unintentionally communicate their expectations for learning to students through actions they take while delivering instruction, as well as interacting with and providing feedback to students. Some of the unintentional messages that are communicated come from the teacher's own beliefs about students and their ability to achieve. Data collected during the Equal Opportunity in the Classroom project showed discrepancies in how teachers treated students based on their perception of the students' abilities (Kerman, 1979). This project, later to be known as the Teacher Expectations and Student Performance (TESA) study, has been used in education programs across the country to illustrate the harmful impact of those unintended messages. Findings showed that teachers were less supportive of students they perceived as low achievers in comparison to students they perceived as high achievers (Kerman, 1979). Examples included that teachers called on those perceived as low achievers less frequently, asked lower-level

DOI: 10.4324/9781003321798-9

questions of them, gave less wait time for their responses, and showed less personal interest in them. These same teacher behaviors can still be seen in many of our current classrooms and undermine the idea that all students are expected to learn at high levels.

At some point in our lives, we have all been influenced by someone else's expectations of us. We may have doubted our skills or talents based on feedback or had our confidence bolstered as a result of encouragement from people in our lives whom we value and respect. Just as those expectations impacted us, they also have an impact on our ghosts. Ghosting is a product of the low expectations of others and of the ghosts themselves that manifest in a negative way and leads to disengagement and dropping out.

A national survey conducted of public school teachers and principals aimed to gather data on their perceptions of student achievement and of students who dropped out of high school (Bridgeland et al., 2009). Results indicated that fewer than 32% of teachers believed that all students should be expected to achieve the same high academic standards or graduate with the skills to do college-level work. Further, only 32% of teachers believed that providing extra support would help struggling students reach those high standards. This study also revealed that 59% of teachers were in favor of separate curriculum paths with lower academic standards for students who were identified as being on a non-college track. Data also showed that 75% of teachers "did not believe students at risk of dropping out would work harder if more were demanded of them – higher academic standards, more studying, and homework – to earn a diploma" (p. 4).

This perception from teachers was contradictory to research that found 66% of students who dropped out stated "they would have worked harder if more had been demanded of them in the classroom" (Bridgeland et al., 2006, p. 3). Students also indicated they had increased confidence in their academic ability when their teachers set higher expectations, while also ensuring they had the support and guidance to succeed (Bridgeland et al., 2010). This confirmed research that suggested teacher interest and support would increase a student's desire to remain in school (Wehlage & Rutter, 1985). Students who perceived that their teachers expected them to drop out did so at a higher rate than those students who perceived teachers expected them to finish (Dalton et al., 2009).

Remote learning was less than ideal for the majority of students and resulted in students making less academic progress as compared to learning in person (Kane, 2022). It was an accepted reality that students would be behind in their learning, but teaching students who are performing below grade level is not something that is unique to experienced educators. It just seems that as a result of remote learning and pandemic protocols, there are now more students who are behind. But lowering expectations or trying to "intervention" our way out of this is not the solution. It also is not the time for us to forgo instruction that challenges our students. While that may be tempting after evaluating what students achieved during remote learning, what is best for our students is actually raising expectations and employing strategies that increase their rate of learning (Bambrick-Santoyo & Chiger, 2021). By identifying the teacher behaviors that can communicate low expectations and adopting different high-expectation strategies, we can make up for the learning time that was lost and impact how students may view themselves and their ability.

Communicating High Expectations for ALL

As I provide support to different schools and districts across the country, the topic of student performance is often a focus of conversations. Whether I am meeting with a leadership team, a grade-level team, or engaging with individual teachers in their classrooms, the discussion usually turns to pointing out a single student or to categorizing small groups of students. Statements like "They are the tier 3 kids", "He's special ed", "She is the GATE", or "They don't speak English" are some of the most common I hear. Unfortunately, students sometimes overhear those same conversations as teachers talk to each other in the hallways, lunch room, and in the teachers' workroom.

Discussions also take place between teachers throughout the school year as they share, sometimes out of frustration, about the current achievement of students in a certain class and forecast what teachers can expect from their upcoming class. Comments like "This year's fourth graders are so good; you will love having them"; "These kindergarteners are wild"; or "This eighth-grade group has the most F's" set teachers up with an expectation that may alter how they build relationships and design instructional experiences based on how those comments either raise or lower their expectations of students. In "The Legacy of *Pygmalion in the Classroom*," the authors emphasize "That seemingly innocent banter of the teachers' lounge may be converted into expectations that have a profound impact on children's success" (Dworkin & Dworkin, 1979, p. 712) and "Expectation is a symptom of classification, not evaluation" (p. 712). Even though we all assume we start the year determined to not let these types of comments influence us, they invariably do if we are not mindful that children grow and change throughout the school year and through the summer months. So, those labels another teacher gives them might be inaccurate.

In their book *What Is It About Me You Can't Teach?*, Eleanor Rodriguez and James Bellanca (2017) write that teachers with high expectations believe all students can learn at high levels, and given the opportunity and support, all students can think critically and apply their learning. Mastering and applying high-level skills and thinking requires practice in the classroom. Lessons must include not only strategies and protocols for how students will practice, but also the specific teacher actions that will support students as they learn. In this section, we will review strategies that, when used effectively, will raise academic expectations for ALL students. While this list could be quite lengthy, we will focus on relatively simple changes that have an immediate and dramatic impact. These strategies are also linked to topics covered in earlier chapters and provide leverage in multiple areas. As you reflect on how each can be applied in your own classroom, also consider how you might approach each with more intent to clearly communicate your high expectations.

Total Participation

Throughout most of my time in the classroom, the requirement to raise a hand and wait to be called on before responding was memorialized in my classroom rules and on my course syllabus. At best, I was inconsistent with enforcement; at worst, I ignored it completely. As a high school physics teacher, there were many days that I was just excited to have any student respond, even if they were shouting out. After some gentle reminders and an opportunity to revisit the TESA study, I eliminated that practice. Why? Because it can reinforce low expectations.

Anyone who has ever taught or visited in a kindergarten or first-grade classroom will relate to this scenario (not that it doesn't happen elsewhere, but it is most common here). Teacher gets only the first three words of a prompt spoken, and immediately ten hands fly up into the air. Teacher finishes and then calls on the student whom she believes had a hand up first. Student responds with "I don't remember." Let's process why this response happens. Almost without exception, when students raise their hands, they stop listening. They attempt to hold their responses in their minds and are no longer thinking or processing the complete prompt. If they get distracted by anything, they forget what they had to say. Additionally, when one or more students raise their hands to answer, others who are more reluctant to respond relax and sometimes disengage because they feel covered by those who do have a raised hand. This practice does not reinforce that all students should think and formulate a response, nor does it value all voices in the classroom (Groshell, 2018).

An alternative to calling only on those with raised hands is the use of a random-selection tool like equity sticks. As a reminder, equity sticks, or popsicle sticks, playing cards or computer-generated spinners, are a common tool that teachers use to randomize students who are called on to respond in the classroom. While they do ensure equal opportunity to be recognized to speak, they do not actually promote equity or honor all voices in the classroom. All students should have the opportunity to share their thinking and learning when given a prompt by the teacher.

In Chapter 5, we discussed questioning and academic conversations as a way to increase engagement. Questions that promote critical thinking paired with a structured discussion protocol also communicate high expectations because they provide all students a voice and reinforce considering the ideas of others. As students engage in conversations with their peers, they may be presented with ideas that confirm their own thinking, and they may be challenged to consider an alternative view. In either instance, as they consider how to integrate these perspectives with their own, they are pushed to think more critically. Questions and discussion protocols ensure that no student is deprived of the chance, or better yet the invitation, to learn at high levels. Peer partners or small group discussions also create a safe space for all students to speak, and students who are reluctant to participate in large group discussions are less intimidated. There are often students who question whether their own thinking is correct or valid; others may be anxious to share in a large group. Allowing students to share in a smaller setting first helps to alleviate these types of issues. As a next step, equity sticks or hand raising can be used as a means to deepen the conversation with the whole class. As students practice this routine of thinking, partnering, and sharing with a peer or peers in small groups, the expectation for total participation becomes a normal part of classroom operations, reluctant students more easily join in, and responses from all students are of higher quality.

Open-Ended Performance Tasks

The sense of urgency to "catch up" felt by many teachers since the return from remote learning has caused instruction to occur at a much faster pace and assignments to be more geared toward low-level recall than critical thinking focused. As a result, students have had fewer opportunities to apply what they are learning in the classroom to unique situations, to have a choice in how they show their learning, or to find creative solutions to real-world problems. This, as mentioned earlier, has left students unmotivated and unable to see value in the work they are assigned.

One way to address these issues and to set higher expectations is through the use of open-ended performance tasks. Performance tasks have been a part of assessment design as a way for students to apply their learning. They also foster higher engagement and motivation and serve to deepen understanding

(Ainsworth & Donovan, 2019; Marzano, 2011; McTighe & Gareis, 2021; Reeves, 2020). But many performance tasks currently used in classrooms have a single, predetermined outcome, which translates into every student's work product looking exactly the same. This leaves little to no room for student creativity and eliminates any choice options for demonstrating learning, plus it is really boring to grade. So, the key distinction I want to make is that tasks should be open-ended and allow students the option to show their learning in ways that emphasize their interests and talents. Open-ended performance tasks present students with a relevant situation in which they can use the concepts and skills they are learning in class. They provide enough information to generate a solution but are not so specific as to create a single correct response. The best open-ended performance tasks validate that there can be multiple pathways of getting to a solution or outcome. The criteria for measuring the success of the outcome, though, should be at the same high levels of thinking and skill for all students.

Open-Ended Chemistry Task

Select a chemical reaction that takes place when common household chemicals or products are combined. Construct a paragraph explaining the process by which the chemical reaction occurs including the pertinent scientific laws/theories, periodic trends, and the patterns of chemical properties. Also provide any cautions that would need to be communicated to consumers.

Open-Ended Social Studies Task

You have been tasked with providing a reporter's account of the events leading up to a significant conflict in our history. You can choose how to develop and describe the outline of events, but the information included must be historically accurate. Your means of communication might be a news article, a live report, an infographic, or another of your choosing.

Success Criteria

If the goals are to increase students' probability of success on tasks and for our expectations to be clear, then developing and sharing success criteria with students is vital. Success criteria, simply defined, are the required elements for students to include in their work and make it clear to students the evidence that is required to show they have achieved the intended learning outcome (Almarode & Vandas, 2019). As a result, students are better able to produce quality work and show deeper understanding. One negative perception some teachers have shared with me regarding the use of success criteria is that this lowers expectations by giving students too much information or they give away the answer. Success criteria, when developed correctly, are not a fill-in-the-blank process or just re-copying an example. To me, it is the difference between giving students the steps or directions to drive themselves to the destination and me doing the driving for them. Students need to be able to find their way to the target location (quality work), and they all should have the requirements needed to get there successfully.

When success criteria are used effectively in the classroom, they help students monitor their own progress toward the intended learning target. They are better equipped to self-assess where they are in their work and know what they need to do next. Success criteria not only help students understand the steps they need to take to accomplish a task but also provide focus and clarity for how their work will be judged (Fisher & Frey, 2018). Whether written in the form of "I can" statements or as specific details on a rubric, success criteria clearly communicate the expected learning for all students. And as an added bonus, success criteria translate easily to rubrics making it easier to provide specific feedback for improvement (Gonzalez, 2015).

Models of Exemplary Work

As students work on their tasks, they should understand how using success criteria translates into a quality work product. Exemplary work (exemplars) provides students with a way to self-assess, peer-assess, and better understand teacher feedback for improvement. Exemplars provide both teachers and students with a model for comparison. Just like success criteria provide

Success Criteria Examples

"I can" Statements

- ◆ I can use fractions to make equal parts of a whole.
- ◆ I can identify the main idea in a paragraph.
- ◆ I can distinguish between photosynthesis and respiration.

Specific Details

- ◆ Identifies the information needed/used for making a claim
- ◆ Cites evidence from two sources to support an argument
- ◆ Accurately measures the area of a polygon and includes mathematical calculations

the steps, exemplars provide the road map. The development of exemplars also provides the teacher or a colleague the opportunity to follow the same directions given to students to be sure they lead to the expected outcome (Reeves, 2020).

Using a fourth-grade standard, the example below is a model for how success criteria are used with an open-ended performance task. Please note that this model would be used with students to show the work that is expected. The actual problem I would give them would be different, but the success criteria would be the same.

High expectations tell students that we believe in them and their ability to learn. We communicate high expectations to students when we provide them with tasks that challenge them to think at high levels, we share the criteria for success, and we give them models of quality work. Students are then able to see value in the work they are asked to do, are motivated to complete it, are more engaged in the learning process, and have greater confidence in their ability to meet high expectations.

Example: Open-Ended Task, Success Criteria, and Exemplar

Standard

Find factors and multiples of numbers in the range 1–100.

(a) Find all factor pairs for a given whole number.
(b) Recognize that a whole number is a multiple of each of its factors.

Performance Task:

Lori's mother needs her to help out on their peach farm. For ease with inventory, she wants Lori to distribute 36 peaches equally into baskets. She will use more than 1 but fewer than 10 baskets. How many baskets does Lori need to accomplish this task? Using words, numbers and pictures, show two ways to do this and explain how you found your answer. Include in your response…

Success Criteria:

1. A drawing that shows the number of baskets needed and the number of peaches in each.
2. An equation/number sentence that shows how you calculate your answer.
3. Label appropriate multiples and/or factors.
4. Write word sentences to state your answers, explain how you found your answers using appropriate vocabulary (for example, multiple, factor, and factor pair) and how you know your answers are correct.

Exemplar

6 baskets with 6 peaches in each total 36 peaches.

factor   factor   multiple
  6   ×   6   =   36
6 is a factor of 36. 36 is a multiple of 6 and 6.

factor   factor   multiple
  4   ×   9   =   36
4 baskets with 9 peaches in each total 36 peaches.
4 and 9 are factors of 36. 36 is a multiple of 9 and 4.
I know my answers are correct because there are equal numbers of peaches in each basket.

Power of Believing

> If you feel like somebody thinks you're going to be something, you're going to have confidence. Just like if somebody thinks you're pretty, and they tell you all the time you're pretty, you're going to think you're pretty. You need people there for you that are going to encourage you to do good. [Teachers] need to be there for you for you to feel like you can do it.
>
> (Freeland, 2013, pp. 125–126)

The quote above was captured from a conversation with a young lady who was participating in an alternative dropout prevention program. She began ghosting as she was struggling to manage caring for a new baby while also trying to complete course requirements for graduation. She shared that it was the encouragement and support she received from her teachers that made her believe she could overcome her current situation, persevere, and ultimately finish high school.

Most of us have had an experience with someone complimenting, supporting, or encouraging us. Maybe it had to do with our appearance, a work product, or a performance. We can identify with this positive feeling and the boost in confidence it provides. We probably have also experienced the opposite feeling that accompanies criticism. Believing you are capable or that you have the skills or talents to be successful in accomplishing a task is what we know as self-efficacy, and it is powerful in boosting confidence and motivation to continue even in the face of failure. When self-efficacy is absent, we are more likely to avoid a task or question its value because we feel we will not complete it successfully (Doménech-Betoret et al., 2017).

In her work on mindsets, Carol Dweck (2006) shares "The view you adopt for yourself profoundly affects the way you lead your life" (p. 6). She discusses the impact on learning for those who believe their abilities are what they are and cannot be changed (fixed mindset) and those who believe that abilities can be changed through effort (growth mindset). These mindsets influence their motivation and how they approach risk taking. Students who consistently receive failing grades and do not meet academic standards often view themselves through a fixed mindset. These students tend to disregard feedback because they feel additional effort will not matter as this is just who they are and what they are capable of as a student. They do not accept that they have the ability to change how much they can accomplish as a learner if they just keep trying (Rhew et al., 2018). Students who operate from a growth mindset and believe it is within their control to learn more achieve at higher levels and also have higher levels of self-efficacy (Dweck & Masters, 2009).

In the hallway of a small rural school, students in a third-grade class could be heard chanting with enthusiasm and conviction, "If I believe it, I can achieve it!" They have the good fortune of being in the classroom with yet another skilled ghost whisperer. After their morning work and calendar routines are completed, their teacher signals the start of the academic day with that choral recitation. It goes on for at least a minute as they exclaim it over and over. The energy in the room as they start to review and learn new things is high, and the students are eager to participate in all that the teacher asks of them. This teacher and her students are in a school that is 100% minority and 100% poverty, but her students perform at high levels akin to those schools in more affluent areas. She is an anomaly in her school because of her ghost whispering skills. She believes her students are capable of high academic achievement, she expects them to do well, and she makes sure the students believe and expect it of themselves. She is a model for how we can create an environment that quells ghosting and allows students to believe they can be successful.

Part 2 Key Points and Reflection Journal

- ◆ Relationships are the main drivers connecting students to school and to learning. When students feel they are seen, valued, and belong, they are more academically successful.
- ◆ When we invite students into the learning with questions and the opportunity to share ideas, we move them from being passive to active in the learning process.
- ◆ There are many ways that teachers intentionally and unintentionally communicate expectations to students. When high expectations are held for all students and are evident in the classroom, students' beliefs in their abilities and capacity to grow intellectually, their self-efficacy, is greater.

Do Now:

Communicating High Expectations
1. What unintentional behaviors do you exhibit that actually communicate low expectations?
2. What behaviors will you adopt, adapt, or abandon to intentionally communicate high expectations for all students?
3. Complete the following sentence.
I have high expectations for my students, and I make that known _____.

Reflection:

One idea that was new or presented a different perspective…
I now think differently about…
For the next steps, I will try…
I want to learn more about…

Part 3

Closing the Gateway – How Can We Shut Down the Pathway to Ghosting?

Creating the Conditions

In the Netflix series *Stranger Things*, we are introduced to the Upside Down, a parallel world that exists underneath the surface of Earth. The Upside Down mirrors the surface world in composition (geography, buildings, and roadways) but is different in that it is a scary place devoid of security, happiness, and the safety net of the important people in our lives. The Upside Down is dark and sometimes foggy which makes it hard to see your surroundings. It preys on fear and insecurity and also is an energy drain due to the psychological stress it creates. It can make you feel isolated, scared, and hopeless. There are multiple gateways to the Upside Down, as it is very connected to people and places on the surface. Sometimes it is accessed by a personal choice to enter, and other times the Upside Down exerts an involuntary force that pulls the mind and consciousness there. Because bad things happen in the Upside Down, there is a constant quest to close the gateway and halt the physical and mental movement back and forth.

DOI: 10.4324/9781003321798-10

For some students, classrooms are like the Upside Down. Feeling psychologically or physically unsafe in these spaces can fuel the fear, anxiety, uncertainty, and disconnection that inhibit students from learning and being successful. Whether there is a real or perceived threat of bullying, ridicule, or physical harm, the stress caused by these feelings leaves students unable to access the parts of their brain needed to take in and process information (Willis, 2014). When the brain is in a state of stress, students are unable to focus their attention, manage classroom routines or procedures, or control their emotions (Van Marter Souers & Hall, 2020). The brain switches to survival mode, and the fight-or-flight instinct shuts down the ability to learn.

In the years prior to the COVID-19 pandemic, much focus was placed on creating safe and inclusive environments for all students. Social-emotional learning and trauma-informed practices became a part of daily instruction to address the non-academic competencies needed for success both inside and outside of the classroom (Goodwin, 2018). These non-academic competencies (i.e., emotional control, perseverance, empathy, growth mindset, and resilience) help students better manage those factors that pull their attention and raise the brain's stress levels. Schools were making strides in providing support to those students who bring heavy personal baggage into the building each day to subvert the impact it has on their physical and mental health. Unfortunately, none of us could have imagined or predicted what would happen to students in March of 2020 when we shifted to remote learning and put them in the Upside Down of online learning.

Many of our students live in high-stress situations, and the pandemic shutdown only served to worsen stress at home. Parents and care-givers lost employment and income; family members and friends became sick and passed away; civil unrest plagued cities and communities; and while all of this was taking place, students were isolated from their peers, teachers, and daily routines and support structures (Furfaro, 2021). During the time students were in remote learning, nearly 78% of teens reported some barrier to performing well in school ("Students Weigh In, Part III", 2021). Of those students, 49% reported being depressed, stressed, or anxious. As a result of remote learning, academic growth was hindered because students simply did not have the brain control needed to make learning happen.

After returning to in-person schooling, we learned the effects of distractions, disruptions, and stressors left students with brains that were changed, and we are yet to know the extent (Furfaro, 2021). There is also a significant indication that pandemic stressors more greatly impacted students from lower-income homes and students who were already at risk. These changes are evident not only in students' academic progress, but also in their behaviors. Many schools have seen dramatic increases in "meltdown" behaviors from students because their brains are simply not able to regulate their emotions. The good news is, we have the ability to reverse this change. There are structures and processes we can put in place in the classroom to reduce brain stress and foster the feeling of safety students need to reconnect with the parts of the brain that allow them to learn (Willis, 2014).

To create the conditions that students now need, we have to consider factors that reduce brain stressors in the classroom. By developing consistent progressions of classroom procedures and expectations, working intentionally to foster and restore hope, and confronting detrimental policies, we can close the gateway that pulls students away both mentally and physically. In Chapter 7, we explore how teacher teams can reduce confusion and anxiety through common processes and expectations. Chapter 8 highlights the importance of hope as an avenue to perseverance and confidence for learner success, and Chapter 9 examines district and school policies that pose barriers to halting the ghosting process. It is up to us to tackle the additional factors that keep the gateway open and allow more ghosts to be lost.

Let's kick out the doorstop!

7

Call in Reinforcements – How Can Teacher Teams Face Down the Ghosting Challenge Together?

You Have Been Selected

As educators, very few of us have escaped the opportunity to work with or be a part of a team. Many of us have received the "You have been selected" email informing us that we were chosen for specialized work within our schools. Whether we volunteered or were "volun-told," we most likely have had numerous occasions to collaborate with colleagues and problem solve as a team. In most of these instances, there is a task at hand to be completed. Whether writing the school improvement plan, planning a field trip, organizing a fundraiser, or planning an instructional sequence, we know how to focus to get things done.

During remote learning, teacher teaming became a challenge. The divide between classrooms and colleagues was vast, and online collaboration and professional learning of any sort were not highly effective because extended daily screen time was exhausting. New technologies had to be learned and unfamiliar programs were introduced during this time, so teacher

DOI: 10.4324/9781003321798-11

collaboration mostly centered on the set up and management of these tools. Little time was available to discuss effective strategies for remote teaching, even though we all learned valuable skills and strategies as we navigated the virtual environment. Now that we have returned in person, re-establishing the relationships and trust needed to function as effective teams has taken additional time, but it is necessary to rebuild our teams.

We sometimes find it difficult to work together on common classroom practices to support students. We have become so accustomed to closing ourselves off in our own classrooms that we struggle to come to agreement with others about how we might best serve all students (Reeves & DuFour, 2016). Sadly, many of our grade-level and department meetings are more about coordination than true collaboration. Within all of the schools I have served, the use of the language of Professional Learning Communities (PLCs) is common. Almost every teacher is familiar with the four questions that guide PLC work and can agree on what students should learn and how it will be assessed, but rarely do I see a commitment to every teacher taking collective responsibility for the learning of all students (Reeves & DuFour, 2016). If supporting all learners is our goal, then our focus must then be on not just what we want students to know, how we will know if they know, what we will do if they already know, and what we will do if they don't know, but also on how students will come to know, a point that is not included in those essential four questions. Collective responsibility requires a deep commitment to our students and to the colleagues on our team. This commitment moves us beyond data collection and analysis of what students are learning to identifying and addressing the learning needs of those within our classrooms. It is this additional emphasis that takes us deeper with the examination of those strategies that have the greatest impact on learning (Venables, 2019).

When we, as a team, believe that we have a greater impact on the learning of students than the factors that influence them outside of the classroom, we have what is called collective efficacy (DeWitt, 2019). To effectively examine our impact and build collective efficacy, we must be willing to collect data on the *results* of our teaching (student work samples and assessments), as well as data on the *methods* of our teaching (specific instructional strategies and with what frequency). Looking at both the causes (teaching) and effects (learning) enables us to build on those practices that facilitate the most academic growth and eliminate those practices that inhibit gains. Fully engaging in the PLC process makes us more effective and efficient as a team and as individual teachers.

Too often within our teams, we align ourselves with those who have similar philosophies and practices to our own (Herrmann, 2019). We search for opportunities to affirm what we already believe and do within our classrooms. As we consider the gifts and talents of our team members, we would be well served to remember that everyone brings something unique to the table due to our different approaches and experiences with students. Psychiatrist Carl Jung held that "Everyone you meet knows something you don't know but need to know. Learn from them." Our commitment to collective responsibility and learning for all means we embrace the opportunity to learn from and with each other. We value all members, and therefore, consider different perspectives and possibilities. Whether we are sharing different views on the writing process or strategies for academic conversations, everyone has something to contribute. In *Cooperation or Collaboration,* we are reminded that "we stand to learn the most from people who differ from us" (Hermann, 2019, para. 13). Embracing teaming will help us leverage the gift and talents of others for the benefit of our students, especially our ghosts.

Teaming for Transition

Students experience many transitions as they move through their years of schooling, and each transition presents both new opportunities and new stresses. These transitions include moving from home to school, elementary to middle school, middle to high school, and high school to college or the work force. For some, these transitions come with a change in buildings, which adds the additional stress of learning to navigate a new location.

For young children, moving from preschool or home to kindergarten is one of the most significant transitions they will encounter in their schooling. They experience a change in place, new expectations, adjustment to a new peer group, unfamiliar authority figures, and a new role as a student. During this first year, they adjust to routines that teach them how to be at school and begin to learn how to learn. It can be highly stressful for many students to follow a set schedule and routine that is very different from what they were accustomed to at home. Younger students also enter school with high variability in their preschool and home experiences, which poses great challenges for teachers to determine where they are in their social-emotional and academic learning. Kindergarten sets the stage for all the years that follow, so it is critical that students have the support they need to be successful (Burkam & Lee, 2002).

Moving from elementary school to middle school presents a different set of struggles resulting in consistent student achievement loss. This loss is partly attributed to the transition from self-contained classrooms in elementary schools to multiple classrooms in middle-level schools (Alspaugh & Harting, 1995). Students can have difficulties with the changes in academic demands, having to navigate larger schools with a larger population, being accountable to different teachers in each subject, while at the same time going through physiological, emotional, and social changes. School zoning patterns often force students to leave behind one group of friends to mix with a new group. These factors make it difficult for students to find where they belong and meet all of the different expectations that are set for them.

The passage of students from the middle grades to high school is the most difficult transition point in education. The failure rate in grade nine is three to five times higher than that of any other grade (Bragg et al., 2002). Ninth grade has the highest discipline rates, retention rates, truancy rates, and failure rates (Habeeb et al., 2008). It is the foundational year for most high schools and is also the year when successful habits are developed. This is also the time we see the greatest formation of ghosts. Many students do not have the ability to look ahead and see how the decisions they make in eighth and ninth grade will impact their future success. And, because credits for graduation begin accumulating in ninth grade, course selections made by rising eighth graders are critical. Think about what students experienced during pandemic learning. Many students were at home on remote learning during these critical transition years and are now struggling to catch up socially, mentally, and academically (Bagnall et al., 2022). The absence of structured transition programs leaves so many students in the Upside Down without the connections or skills to find their way out.

Successfully transitioning students is not just a one-day or one-week endeavor and should be a process that scaffolds support for students each year. Effective teams can set students up for success by establishing common procedures and expectations, and collaboration is needed to continue through to the next successive grade levels. Grade-level transition should not be just a set of activities that take place at the beginning of the year but a process that is incorporated throughout the school year. The planning for these transitions should include communication with parents to understand home routines that might be incorporated into the start of the kindergarten year that can support the change in environment. As students transition to middle the middle grades, vertical teaming with the previous grade can help determine practices could be scaffolded throughout the year instead of them just abruptly changing. And, those same vertical conversations should take place as students move from the middle grades to high school. Including common routines and procedures from the previous year to start students out with something familiar will set them up for success and provide teachers a baseline to move them forward.

By developing a successful transition program, students will gain the knowledge, tools, skills, and dispositions to do well. Strong communication between sending and receiving grades and schools throughout the year fosters collective responsibility and smooth transition procedures. When teacher teams develop common expectations and meet periodically to identify common problems and discuss solutions, they are able to help students understand and cope successfully with the challenges of transition and to experience academic success (Habeeb et al., 2008). In other words, they, as a team, are able to slow the ghosting process.

Teaming Our Expectations

Imagine it is your first day at a new job. Every hour on the hour, you meet a new supervisor who is in charge of monitoring your work, and each of them explains the tasks and behavioral expectations they have for you. As you move through your day, you discover that each supervisor has a different set of requirements you must manage each hour of every day. The materials you need to work with each hour are different. You must use specific colors of ink for different tasks. Different types of paper are needed for each task. There are different procedures for how to ask questions or speak to co-workers. At the end of the day, your head would be swimming to remember all of the details for each segment of your day. Now imagine that you are 15 years old, and it is the first day of the new school year.

Each year millions of students return to school excited to see their friends, to meet their teachers, and to find out what the new year will hold for them. Teachers typically spend the bulk of the time on the first day on rules, procedures, and materials management. After hearing different procedures and rules from multiple teachers, students end the day overwhelmed and worried about making mistakes. More time is spent outlining compliant behaviors than on helping students develop habits of success that they can strengthen from one year to the next (Scanfeld et al., 2018). Now imagine how less overwhelmed students would be if common expectations and procedures were established and scaffolded across classrooms and grade levels.

An effective way to support students and their learning in the classroom is the development and use of common procedures and expectations (Habeeb et al., 2008). In Chapter 6, we discussed the importance of high expectations and how they can be communicated. Let's now envision how common expectations, when taught and used consistently within and across grade levels, can increase learning. Establishing common expectations and procedures helps to lower stress levels for students while also providing support throughout each day. When support is scaffolded to be greatest at the beginning of the year while students are learning the new procedures and expectations and then decreases toward the end of the year after they have been internalized, students are better able to focus on learning the desired content.

There are many different areas within the classroom where we establish procedures and expectations to help us get things done effectively and efficiently. What follows next are two key areas to consider for developing and scaffolding common expectations and procedures, along with why this is beneficial.

Required Materials

Before and after the first day of school, students and parents spend a lot of time and money trying to buy all of the different materials teachers require for daily classroom use. A student may need a composition notebook for English class, loose-leaf paper for math, a spiral notebook for science, red ink pens, blue ink pens, mechanical pencils, etc. Managing what to bring or when to have it is stressful. It is no wonder we constantly have students showing up to class having forgotten something in their lockers or at home. Consider how, as a team, we can come to an agreement on common materials and how students will be expected to manage them. Think about what might be kept in the classroom as opposed to in desks, lockers, or at home. Some teacher teams adopt a single three-ring binder system and other folder systems. Whatever your team deems most appropriate is fine, as long as it is used consistently across classrooms. Also consider more latitude given at the beginning of the year and tapering down throughout the year. Maybe more grace to go back to a locker is given at the start of school than at the end of December, and even less in March. As I heard Dr. Adoph Brown say at a 2022 conference in Utah, "Children don't change overnight;

they change over time." Scaffolding across the year allows for opportunities to learn, change, and get better.

Standard Operating Procedures

All teachers have differing views and beliefs about accepting late work from students, and, in the aftermath of remote learning, whether work is submitted on paper or online. Some teachers believe that penalties for late work are necessary, while others are willing to award the credit earned for completion. Some teachers allow retakes on assignments and assessments; some drop the lowest scores. Wherever you are in your beliefs, know that students can receive conflicting and confusing messages when each teacher has a different requirement. These differing messages also result in more class time required to review procedures and less time for teaching and learning.

Developing common procedures is a simple way to lessen confusion and stress for teachers and students. When teachers support each other across classrooms and students only have one set of procedures to follow, the likelihood that they will be followed or met increases dramatically, and lowered anxiety means students can focus on learning and not compliance (Habeeb et al., 2008). We should also take time to teach and model what we want from students. We should never assume that students will just "know" what we want from them, especially after three years of interrupted schooling. If both academic growth is our goal, then reducing the stress caused by managing differing expectations and procedures will free up the brain functioning needed to make that happen.

Teaming for Success

Henry Ford is credited with saying, "Coming together is a beginning, staying together is progress, and *working together* is success." Whether we are focused on common curricular goals or common classroom procedures and expectations, teaming provides greater support for our students and creates an environment in which they can better focus on learning.

Do Now:

Leveraging Teamwork

1. Does your grade level, subject area, or department currently meet as a team?
2. What is the focus of your meeting time?
3. How do you transition students from one grade level to the next?
4. Do you have common expectations and procedures or are they different between classrooms?
5. What commitments will you make as a team to support and transition students?
6. How will you and your team accept collective responsibility for their success?

8

Instilling Hope – How Can We Instill Hope in Our Ghosts and Help Them Create a Vision of Their Future?

Losing Hope

The Upside Down constantly feeds on the insecurities held by those with whom it is connected. Whether those negative feelings are from trauma, sadness, or guilt, they are used as fuel for self-doubt and anxiety until all hope is lost. But those who can conjure up positive thoughts of love, happiness, and safety can escape the pull of the Upside Down.

Many of our students come to us already suffering from feelings of hopelessness. Some of those feelings come from traumatic experiences at home, and many of our students feel hopeless from repeatedly being unsuccessful at school. Feelings of hopelessness grew during remote learning from over 36% reporting those feelings prior to the pandemic to over 44% of students (Smith, 2022). It was also reported that 71% of students said that school work made them feel anxious or depressed because

DOI: 10.4324/9781003217022-12

completing it was more difficult due to less support from their teachers (National 4-H Council, 2020; Smith, 2022). When students lack hope, they can feel stuck and unable to problem solve. As hopelessness overtakes all positive emotions, students begin to withdraw. They become disengaged and overwhelmed, and they cannot envision what the future may hold for them (Fleming, 2021).

In *Hope Rising: How the Science of Hope Can Change Your Life*, hope is defined as "the belief that your future can be brighter and better than your past and that you actually have a role to play in making it better" (Gwinn & Hellman, 2018, p. 9). Fortunately, evidence suggests that hope can be shared with others and is a learnable skill (Fleming, 2021; Lopez, 2014). This can be a game changer for students' academic success.

> Researchers have found that students who are high in hope have greater academic success, stronger friendships, and demonstrate more creativity and better problem-solving. They also have lower levels of depression and anxiety and are less likely to drop out from school.
>
> (Zakrzewski, 2012, para. 4)

Relationships between teachers and students, as discussed in Chapter 4, forge the way to positive mindsets and the ability to set goals, and goal setting is the first step to a better future. Chapter 3 suggests having students share their story as a way for us to know them better. Imagine if they also wrote their future story. When students can envision their future selves, they can begin to plot the course for that future.

Goal setting, identifying problem-solving strategies, and motivation all come from a place of hope, and as teachers, we are dispensers of hope (Patrick & Peery, 2021). What we say and do in the classroom each day can instill greater hope in our students. Our choice to build strong relationships with our students, to carefully monitor how we communicate our expectations, and to use fair and equitable practices creates an environment that helps our students have hope and be able to write their future stories. When students have hope, they have "goals, the motivation to pursue them, and the determination to overcome obstacles and find pathways to achieve them" (Gwinn & Hellman, 2018, p. xvi).

Restoring Hope

One of the most important things we can do for our ghosts is to create pathways for them to see that success in school is a possibility. When students repeatedly experience failure, they reach the point that they no longer want to engage in the learning process. As teachers, we have the ability to change the cycle of failure by employing simple strategies that can restore hope. By helping students see that they can change their path to reach a different outcome, we foster their motivation to try. In the sections that follow, we will look at classroom practices that have a high impact on restoring hope.

Proportionate Grading Scale

One of the significant impacts from school closures and remote learning is the increased number of students who are struggling academically, and this is resulting in more course and grade-level failures. Many of these low grades are because of missing or incomplete assignments, which means more zeros have been added to the gradebook. One simple and effective way to address failure rates and restore hope to students is to examine our grading scale. Most teachers use some traditional form of averaging system that applies the 100-point scale. When you consider that the 100-point scale includes more levels of failure than of passing, it is no wonder that we have higher levels of students who are failing.

| 0 | 10 | 20 | 30 | 40 | 50 | 60 | 70 | 80 | 90 | 100 |

Think about what it would mean if we changed to a four-point scale or simply set our minimum grade to 50. By making this simple change, we give the 0-F/failure category equal weighting to the levels of passing.

| 0 | 1 | 2 | 3 | 4 |

We have not lowered our requirements or expectations; we have simply corrected a mathematical inequality that disproportionately penalizes students for missing work. One zero can have a dramatic impact on a student's grade. This impact skews grades in a way that can inaccurately reflect what students actually know. Balancing the F with the same weighting as the A-D provides a better depiction of students' learning (Reeves & DuFour, 2016). This one change will have a significant impact on reducing the number of failures and will also restore hope and motivation to those students who need it (Freeland, 2022).

Second Chances

A good half of the friends I grew up with failed their drivers' exam the first time. They all had another opportunity to try again, and they all eventually were licensed to drive. When I did not score as high as I had hoped on my ACT to get into college, I was able to take it again to improve my score. When I forgot to mail my electricity bill one month (before e-pay was available), the power company left my power on and gave me a 10-day grace period to get it paid. With few exceptions, life is filled with second chances.

Another way to support students and restore hope is to provide second chances. Teachers can do this by scheduling make-up days and allowing redos and retakes on important assignments and assessments. If assignments are worth doing, they should be worth doing well. Getting students to finish an assignment shows them that the work is important and teaches perseverance. Letting them off the hook by allowing them not to complete the task or by simply giving them a zero does not teach them responsibility. It communicates to them that the assignment was not that important to their learning to begin with. Because failing grades are often a result of missing work or low-quality work, allowing second chances reinforces the importance of the work that is assigned and also provides an opportunity for students who need it to get additional support (Wormeli, 2011). For second chance options to be successful, there needs to be a designated class period or day for all students to take advantage of the opportunity. Instructions should be developed so students know how to access the work they are missing or that needs to be improved. It is also important that all eligible assignments are graded and the gradebook updated beforehand. Lastly, teachers need to plan structures to provide help and support to those who will need it. There are usually reasons that students do not complete assignments the first time, and most frequently, that is because they need additional support. For those who repeatedly struggle to complete assignments on time, additional interventions may be necessary. Requiring them to do extra practice or attend tutoring before a retake will help to identify those who need extra help and those who are taking advantage of the second chances.

One drawback that teachers often point out when this option is presented is the extra workload it puts on teachers. Allowing redos and retakes on every assignment could definitely be unmanageable. But for those assignments that are of particular importance or are aligned to critical standards, this is an effective way to reinforce the need to fully learn those standards (Wormeli, 2011).

Classwork, Homework, and Feedback

"If we don't get this done in class, you will have to finish it for homework." This is a sentence I have heard spoken too many times to count, and one I have said myself. As a young teacher, I frequently assigned homework to my students. If we did not have the time needed to "cover" all the content that was listed on our pacing guide, I would ask that they complete work at home. Although the research on the effectiveness of homework is mixed and varies by grade level, one thing is certain. Homework inequitably penalizes students who have no support at home and disproportionately impacts our students of poverty (Neason, 2017).

Remote learning gave us all glimpses into the home lives of students. We saw the chaos, heard the noise, and felt the mood. Most of our students did their best to stay connected and do their work. But for some, it was almost impossible. This insight into our students' worlds should give us pause and cause us to reflect on those practices that do not support learning.

The best professional athletes, surgeons, and musicians all get better through constant practice with coaching from experts. What if we better utilized class time for students to do their work with coaching and feedback from the expert in the room – us? For students who have not been successful, feedback for improvement is critical. When we provide feedback instead of just a grade, we communicate to students that learning is not finished (Reeves & DuFour, 2016). When students know how to use success criteria and feedback, they have the means to produce quality work and, therefore, improve their grades. By teaching them to use success criteria (refer to Chapter 6) and coaching them for improvement, we provide a pathway for both hope and motivation.

With more accurate grading scales, multiple opportunities to show success, and practice with feedback, we allow students to be hopeful about their success and they are more motivated to try to improve. As dispensers of hope, creating these experiences should be a priority.

Do Now:

Becoming a Dispenser of Hope

1. Are there students in your class who seem hopeless?
2. Does your current grading scale have more levels of failure than passing?
3. How many missing assignments are currently reflected in your gradebook?
4. What new steps can you take to support students with completing assignments and improving their grades?

9

Blocking the Pathways – How Can We Eliminate the School- and District-Level Policies That Keep the Gateways Propped Open?

Pathways Outside of the Classroom

Because multiple gateways lead to the Upside Down, it is difficult to stop movement back and forth. This same problem exists within schools and districts, as there are gateways to ghosting that are beyond the classroom. As teachers, we are on the front lines and are the ones who see some of them as they open. While we may feel that some aspects are beyond our control, our voices are powerful in identifying the sources of added gateways. Our ghosts need us to be advocates for change. If our mission is to stop the ghosting process, we must examine those factors that provide more gateways to the ghost world.

While no one is intentionally trying to keep the pathways to ghosting open, there are school and district policies that actually help facilitate the process. Ensuring that policies support the success of all students is difficult, but it is imperative to approach this

DOI: 10.4324/9781003217022-13

process by weighing both positive and punitive aspects. If we fail to consider both, we miss opportunities that will serve to redirect their paths and could end up sending them further down the wrong path. From promotion and retention policies to attendance and discipline procedures, we have to reflect on how these policies will impact students throughout their entire K-12 journey.

Almost all states, districts, and schools exercised some flexibility with their policies during remote learning. Relaxed attendance, graduation, and grading requirements were instituted to help keep students on track and on grade level. With all that we learned during this time, it is imperative that we re-examine and reflect on our current policies for their impact on all students. The sections that follow highlight common areas where policies are in conflict with ending ghost creation. This is not an all-inclusive list and should serve as a starting point for your closer examination of local policies that might continue to create ghosts.

Promotion and Retention Policies

Schools and districts must re-examine promotion and retention policies, especially in the early grades because they are often, by mere design, detrimental to student success. If policies allow more than one retention before reaching high school, it is pretty much guaranteed that a student will disengage and not reach graduation. Most state-level enrollment policies set a maximum age at which students can be enrolled as a twelfth grader (*State Education Practices (SEP)*, 2017). If the second retention will put that student beyond that maximum, the policy causes the student to age out before they can reach graduation.

When deciding to retain students in elementary grades, additional academic opportunities must be provided to allow them to catch up with their grade-level peers. The impact of retention was detailed in Part 1. Carefully planned intervention strategies that allow for students to stay with their grade-level peers are most effective, but the interventions offered must be connected with and transferred into use in the classroom with current content. Interventions that are not connected to current learning and are not immediately useful rarely stick. Students will forget the skill that was learned if its usefulness in the classroom has already passed or is too far down the road.

Intervention

Intervention should be classified as a service and not a place-ment. All students need intervention support at some point during the school year, whether it is the simple review of the organization of the periodic table, extra time to master exposi-tory writing, or re-teaching to understand mathematical iden-tities. Although most schools and districts employ universal screening tools, the misconception that only students who fall below a particular cut score should get help leaves many other students in need without additional time and support for learn-ing (Sparks, 2015). Instead, interventions should be focused in the classroom and target specific skills and concepts that are currently of importance. Grouping should be flexible and of-the-moment so all students have access when help is needed. Missing a cut score by one or two points should not exclude a student from intervention services.

At-Risk Supports

Structures, processes, and supports aimed at helping at-risk students should undergo closer scrutiny to ensure they are maximized so students meet their goals and are academically successful. Oftentimes, the offerings for support are designed to accommodate the adults in the building, and they do not actually meet the needs of the students who need them most. I constantly told my students that I was available to them for help both before and after school. All they had to do was come to my classroom. What I did not realize was that most of them, especially those who lived in poverty, rode the bus to school and were not in con-trol of when they arrived and departed. Opportunities such as after-school tutoring or homework help may not be an option for students who rely on school buses or public transportation. For students who excel in areas like the performing arts, changing their placement to an intervention class instead serves to dimin-ish motivation and disconnection, as the intervention now seems like punishment. Teachers and administrators must constantly examine the support that is offered to students to determine if it is actually helping the targeted population.

Discipline and Attendance Policies

Many school and district policies related to discipline and attendance conflate behavior consequences and academic consequences. Many local policies allow for awarding zeros for work missed while serving a suspension. The suspension is given as the punishment for the behavior, but the student is also receiving an academic punishment. Likewise, there are attendance policies on the books nationwide that state credit can be lost or a student retained if they miss more than ten days in a semester. Punitive policies such as these should be closely examined for their effectiveness. We know that students need to be in attendance to learn, so it is important that schools and districts not overly restrict access to learning. These policies should also be reviewed for the potential to inequitably impact one demographic group over another.

Disengagement starts in the classroom and is also impacted by policies and procedures outside of the classroom. As teachers, we may not have been a part of what is currently in place, but we can use our voices to influence how things are implemented moving forward. Shutting down all of the pathways to ghosting requires an all-hands-on-deck approach and a willingness to confront those policies and procedures that keep those pathways open.

Do Now:

Reviewing School and District Policies

1. What policies and procedures currently conflate behavioral and academic consequences?
2. How do you and your team identify which students are behind their grade-level peers?
3. How are intervention opportunities designed to support all students?
4. What next steps will you take to rally your team to stop the ghosting process?

Reflection:

One idea that was new or presented a different perspective…
I now think differently about…
For the next steps, I will try…
I will ask my team to…
I want to learn more about…

Part 3 Key Points and Reflection Journal

◆ We are more effective at keeping ghosts connected and engaged when we utilize common routines, procedures, and strategies across classrooms.
◆ Hope is a trait that is critical for success and can be learned. When students have hope, they can create a pathway for their future.
◆ School and district policies sometimes keep the pathways to ghosting open. It is imperative, especially post-COVID, that we re-examine their impact on all students.

Closing Thoughts

We have a ghost problem in our schools. We have strategies and tools at our disposal to reconnect with them and re-engage them in learning. To quote educator and the pioneer of effective schools research, Ron Edmunds (1979),

> We can, whenever and wherever we choose, successfully teach all children whose schooling is of interest to us. We already know more than we need to in order to do that. Whether or not we do it must finally depend upon how we feel about the fact that we haven't so far.

Ideas and strategies shared within the preceding chapters are not new or unique but put in the proper context, they can change learning experiences for students. When we approach relationships, engagement, and expectations with intention, team with our colleagues to scaffold common expectations, instill hope in the hopeless, and confront those things that serve to keep pathways open, we can shut down the gateways that draw students away to the ghost world.

Let's turn our ghosts into graduates and re-engage all of those who have disengaged!

References and Resources

Ainsworth, L., & Donovan, K. (2019). *Rigorous Curriculum Design: How to Create Curricular Units of Study That Align Standards, Instruction, and Assessment* (2nd ed.). Rexford, NY: International Center for Leadership in Education.

Alexander, K. L., Entwisle, D. R., & Horsey, C. S. (1997). From First Grade Forward: Early Foundations of High School Dropout. *Sociology of Education*, *70*(2), 87. https://doi.org/10.2307/2673158

Allensworth, E. M., & Easton, J. Q. (2007). *What Matters for Staying On-Track and Graduating in Chicago Public High Schools: A Close Look at Course Grades, Failures, and Attendance in the Freshman Year.* Consortium on Chicago School Research at the University of Chicago. http://ccsr.uchicago.edu/sites/default/files/publications/07%20 What%20Matters%20Final.pdf

Allensworth, E. M., & Easton, J. Q. (2005). *The On-Track Indicator as a Predictor of High School Graduation.* Consortium on Chicago School Research at the University of Chicago. http://ccsr.uchicago.edu/ publications/track-indicator-predictor-high-school-graduation

Almarode, J. T., & Vandas, K. (2019). *Clarity for Learning: Five Essential Practices That Empower Students and Teachers.* Thousand Oaks, CA: Corwin.

Alspaugh, J. W., & Harting, R. D. (1995). Transition Effects of School Grade-Level Organization on Student Achievement. *Journal of Research and Development in Education*, *28*, 145–149. (EJ505828)

Amos, J. (2008). *Dropouts, Diplomas, and Dollars: U.S. High Schools and the Nation's Economy.* Washington, DC: Alliance for Excellent Education. http://all4ed.org/wp content/uploads/2008/08/ Econ2008.pdf

Asmus, M. J. (2017, April 26). *The Neuroscience of Asking Insightful Questions.* Government Executive. https://www.govexec.com/management/ 2017/04/neuroscience-asking-insightful-questions/137274/

Bagnall, C. L., Skipper, Y., & Fox, C. L. (2022). Primary-Secondary School Transition under Covid-19: Exploring the Perceptions and Experiences of Children, Parents/Guardians, and Teachers. *British Journal of Educational Psychology*, *92*(3), 1011–1033. https://doi.org/10.1111/bjep.12485

Bambrick-Santoyo, P., & Chiger, S. (2021, May 7). *After the Pandemic, Schools Can't Hide from "Learning Loss." We Need to Embrace It | Opinion. Newsweek.* https://www.newsweek.com/after-pandemic-schools-cant-hide-learning-loss-we-need-embrace-it-opinion-1589545

Barnum, M. (2022). *Graduation Rates Dip across U.S. as Pandemic Stalls Progress*. Chalkbeat. https://www.chalkbeat.org/2022/1/24/22895461/2021-graduation-rates-decrease-pandemic

Barnum, M., Belsha, K., & Wilburn, T. (2022). *Graduation Rates Dip across U.S. as Pandemic Stalls Progress*. Chalkbeat. https://www.chalkbeat.org/2022/1/24/22895461/2021-graduation-rates-decrease-pandemic

Barton, P. E. (2005). *One-Third of a Nation: Rising Dropout Rates and Declining Opportunities*. Princeton, NJ: Educational Testing Service. Retrieved from http://www.ets.org/Media/Education_Topics /pdf/onethird.pdf

Bayram Özdemir, S., & Özdemir, M. (2020). How Do Adolescents' Perceptions of Relationships with Teachers Change during Upper-Secondary School Years? *Journal of Youth and Adolescence*, *49*(4), 921–935. https://doi.org/10.1007/s10964-019-01155-3

Bragg, D. D., Loeb, J. W., Gong, Y., Deng, C.-P., Yoo, J., & Hill, J. L. (2002). *Transition from High School to College and Work for Tech Prep Participants in Eight Selected Consortia*. Southern Regional Education Board. https://www.sreb.org/publication/transition-high-school-college-and-work-tech-prep-participants-eight-selected-consortia

Breaux, A. L. (2011). *101 "Answers" for New Teachers and Their Mentors* (2nd ed.). New York: Routledge.

Bridgeland, J. M., Balfanz, R., Moore, L. A., & Friant, R. S. (2010). *Raising Their Voices: Engaging Students, teachers, and Parent to Help End the High School Epidemic*. Washington, DC: Civic Enterprises. Retrieved from http://www.civicenterprises.net/MediaLibrary/Docs/raising_their_voices.pdf

Bridgeland, J. M., Dilulio, J. J., & Balfanz, R. (2009). *On the Front Lines of Schools: Perspectives of Teachers and Principals on the High School Dropout Problem.* Civic Enterprises. http://www.att.com/Common/merger/files/pdf/Schools_Front_Lines.pdf

Bridgeland, J. M., Dilulio, J. J., & Morison, K. B. (2006). *The Silent Epidemic: Perspectives of High School Dropouts.* Washington, DC: Civic Enterprises. http://www.silentepidemic.org/pdfs/thesilente pidemic306.pdf

Burkam, D. T., & Lee, V. E. (2002). *Inequality at the Starting Gate.* Economic Policy Institute.

Calvert, S., & Chapman, B. (2022, January 12). Schools See Big Drop in Attendance as Students Stay Away, Citing Covid-19. *Wall Street Journal.* https://www.wsj.com/articles/schools-see-big-drop-in-attendance-as-students-stay-away-citing-covid-19-11641988802

Comer, J. P. (2020). Commentary: Relationships, Developmental Contexts, and the School Development Program. *Applied Developmental Science, 24*(1), 43–47. https://doi.org/10.1080/10888691.2018.1515296

Comer, J. (1995). *Lecture given at Education Service Center.* Houston, TX: Region IV.

Cooper, K. M., Haney, B., Krieg, A., & Brownell, S. E. (2017). What's in a Name? The Importance of Students Perceiving That an Instructor Knows Their Names in a High-Enrollment Biology Classroom. *CBE Life Sciences Education, 16*(1), ar8. https://doi.org/10.1187/cbe.16-08-0265

Curran, C., & the IRIS Center. (2003, 2021). Encouraging Appropriate Behavior. Retrieved from https://iris.peabody.vanderbilt.edu/wp-content/uploads/pdf_case_studies/ics_encappbeh.pdf

Dalton, B., Glennie, E., Ingels, S. J., & Wirt, J. (2009). *Late High School Dropouts: Characteristics, Experiences, and Changes Across Cohorts* (NCES 2009–307). Washington, DC: National Center for Education Statistics, Institute of Education Sciences, U.S. Department of Education. http://nces.ed.gov/pubs2009/2009307.pdf

Davis, B. (2021, December 6). Holding Students Back - An Inequitable and Ineffective Response to Unfinished Learning. *The Education Trust.* https://edtrust.org/resource/holding-students-back-an-inequitable-and-ineffective-response-to-unfinished-learning/

DeWitt, P. (2019, July 1). *How Collective Teacher Efficacy Develops. ASCD.* https://www.ascd.org/el/articles/how-collective-teacher-efficacy-develops

Doménech-Betoret, F., Abellán-Roselló, L., & Gómez-Artiga, A. (2017). Self-Efficacy, Satisfaction, and Academic Achievement: The Mediator Role of Students' Expectancy-Value Beliefs. *Frontiers in Psychology*, *8*, 1193. https://www.frontiersin.org/article/10.3389/fpsyg.2017.01193

Doyle, T. (2011). *Learner Centered Teaching: Putting the Research on Learning into Practice* (1st ed.). Sterling, VA: Stylus Publishing.

Dweck, C. S. (2006). *Mindset: The New Psychology of Success.* New York: Ballantine Books.

Dweck, C., & Master, A. (2009). Self-Theories and Motivation: Student's Beliefs about Intelligence. In K. R. Wentzel & A. Wigfield (Authors), *Handbook of Motivation at School* (pp. 123–140). New York: Routledge.

Dworkin, N., & Dworkin, Y. (1979). The Legacy of "Pygmalion in the Classroom." *The Phi Delta Kappan*, *60*(10), 712–715. https://www.jstor.org/stable/20299573

Edmunds, R. (1979). Effective Schools for the Urban Poor. *Educational Leadership*, *37*(1), 15.

Finn, J. D., & Owings, J. (2006). The Adult Lives of At-Risk Students: The Roles of Attainment and Engagement in High School. (NCES 2006–328). Washington, DC: U.S. Department of Education, National Center for Education Statistics. http://www.cpec.ca.gov/CompleteReports/ExternalDocuments/Adult_Lives_of_At-Risk_Students.pdf

Fisher, L. B. (2020). *Connecting With Reluctant Remote Learners.* Edutopia. https://www.edutopia.org/article/connecting-reluctant-remote-learners

Fisher, D., & Frey, N. (2018, February 1). Show & Tell: A Video Column / A Map for Meaningful Learning. *ASCD.* https://www.ascd.org/el/articles/a-map-for-meaningful-learning

Fleming, N. (2021, March 31). In Schools, Finding Hope at a Hopeless Time. *Edutopia.* https://www.edutopia.org/article/schools-finding-hope-hopeless-time

Freeland, E. (2022). *Reducing Failures – In the Spotlight.* Creative Leadership Solutions. Retrieved June 29, 2022, from https://myemail.constantcontact.com/Reducing-Failures.html?soid=1126630584086&aid=60p8ebB_bql

Freeland, E. S. (2013). The impact of alternative education credit recovery on the academic success of students at risk of dropping out [Unpublished doctoral dissertation]. Samford University.

Furfaro, H. (2021). *Children's brains on stress*. The Hechinger Report. http://hechingerreport.org/childrens-brains-on-stress/

Garnier, H. E., Stein, J. A., & Jacobs, J. K. (1997). The Process of Dropping out of High School: A 19-Year Perspective. *American Educational Research Journal, 34*(2), 395–419. https://doi.org/10.3102/00028312034002395

Goldschmidt, P., & Wang, J. (1999). When Can Schools Affect Dropout Behavior? A Longitudinal Multilevel Analysis. *American Educational Research Journal, 36*(4), 715–738. http://www.jstor.org/stable/1163518

Gonzalez, J. (2015, February 4). Meet the Single Point Rubric. *Cult of Pedagogy*. https://www.cultofpedagogy.com/single-point-rubric/

Goodwin, B. (2018, October 1). Research Matters / SEL: Getting the "Other Stuff" Right. *ASCD*. https://www.ascd.org/el/articles/research-matters-sel-getting-the-other-stuff-right

Groshell, Z. (2018, January 1). Does Hands-up Damage Classrooms? *Education Rickshaw*. https://educationrickshaw.com/2018/01/01/does-hands-up-damage-classrooms/

Gross, B. (2021, February 8). *Analysis: Schools Are Facing a Surge of Failing Grades During the Pandemic — and Traditional Approaches Like Credit Recovery Will Not Be Enough to Manage It*. https://www.the74million.org/article/analysis-schools-are-facing-a-surge-of-failing-grades-during-the-pandemic-and-traditional-approaches-like-credit-recovery-will-not-be-enough-to-manage-it/

Gupta, N., & Reeves, D. B. (2021, December 16). The Engagement Illusion. *ASCD*. https://www.ascd.org/el/articles/the-engagement-illusion

Gwinn, C., & Hellman, C. (2018). *Hope Rising: How the Science of Hope Can Change Your Life*. New York: Morgan James Publishing.

Habeeb, S., Moore, R., & Seibert, A. (2008). *The Ninth Grade Opportunity*. Bloomington, IN: iUniverse, Inc.

Hattie, J. (2017). *Backup of Hattie's Ranking List of 256 Influences and Effect Sizes Related to Student Achievement*. Visible Learning. https://visible-learning.org/backup-hattie-ranking-256-effects-2017/

Helmore, E. (2021, September 18). 'Devious Licks' TikTok Challenge Has Students Vandalising School Bathrooms. *The Guardian*. https://www.

theguardian.com/education/2021/sep/18/devious-licks-tiktok-challenge-vandalism-schools

Herrmann, Z. (2019, July 1). Cooperate or Collaborate? *ASCD*. https://www.ascd.org/el/articles/cooperate-or-collaborate

Hickman, G., Bartholomew, M., Mathwig, J., & Heinrich, R. (2008). Differential Developmental Pathways of High School Dropouts and Graduates. *Journal of Educational Research, 102*(1), 3–14. Retrieved from ERIC database. (EJ809605).

Hollingsworth, H. (2021, May 11). US Schools Fight to Keep Students Amid Fear of Dropout Surge. *ABC News*. https://abcnews.go.com/Health/wireStory/us-schools-fight-students-amid-fear-dropout-surge-77617926

Hoye, J. D., & Sturgis, C. (2005). *A Framework for Dropout Reduction and Recovery*. The Alternative Pathways Project. http://www.nassgap.org/library/docs/alt-pathways.pdf

Hughes, J. N., West, S. G., Kim, H., & Bauer, S. S. (2018). Effect of Early Grade Retention on School Completion: A Prospective Study. *Journal of Educational Psychology*, *110*(7), 974. https://doi.org/10.1037/edu0000243

Hwang, S. H. J., & Cappella, E. (2018). Rethinking Early Elementary Grade Retention: Examining Long-Term Academic and Psychosocial Outcomes. *Journal of Research on Educational Effectiveness*, *11*(4), 559–587. https://doi.org/10.1080/19345747.2018.1496500

Jimerson, S. R., Ferguson, P., Whipple, A. D., Anderson, G. E., & Dalton, M. J. (2002). Exploring the Association between Grade Retention and Dropout: A Longitudinal Study Examining Socio-Emotional, Behavioral, and Achievement Characteristics of Retained Students. *The California School Psychologist*, *7*, 51–62. http://www.education.ucsb.edu/jimerson/retention/CSP_RetentionDropout2002.pdf

Kane, T. (2022, May 22). Kids Are Far, Far Behind in School. *The Atlantic*. https://www.theatlantic.com/ideas/archive/2022/05/schools-learning-loss-remote-covid-education/629938/

Kerman, S. (1979). "Why Did You Call on Me? I Didn't Have My Hand up!" Teacher Expectations and Student Achievement. *The Phi Delta Kappan*, *60*(10), 716–718. https://www.jstor.org/stable/20299574

Lopez, S. J. (2014). *Making Hope Happen: Create the Future You Want for Yourself and Others*. New York: Atria Books.

Marzano, R. J., Pickering, D. J., & Heflebower, T. (2011). *The Highly Engaged Classroom*. Bloomington, IN: Marzano Research Laboratory.

McTighe, J., & Gareis, C. (2021). *Assessing Deeper Learning after a Year of Change*. ASCD. https://www.ascd.org/el/articles/assessing-deeper-learning-after-a-year-of-change?_hsmi=132962103&_hsenc=p2ANqtz-9G8oDISo3i0nmp6Epy5Vj-mRspJyuE3N-3bfLfqswMfBpq7q37OkK_n4fSL7Ky1zgT6ziUb-FyzVFH6sqeB1K-bIFQpDcA

National 4-H Council. (2020, June 17). New Survey Finds 7 in 10 Teens Are Struggling with Mental Health. *4-H*. https://4-h.org/about/blog/new-survey-finds-7-in-10-teens-are-struggling-with-mental-health/

Neason, A. (2017, January 1). Does Homework Help? *ASCD*. https://www.ascd.org/el/articles/does-homework-help

Neild, R. C., & Balfanz, R. (2006). *Unfulfilled Promise: The Dimensions and Characteristics of Philadelphia's Dropout Crisis, 2000–2005*. Philadelphia Youth Network, The Johns Hopkins University, and University of Pennsylvania. http://www.pyninc.org/downloads/Unfulfilled_Promise_Project_U-turn.pdf

No Child Left Behind Act of 2001, P.L. 107–110, 20 U.S.C. § 6319 (2002).

Patrick, P., & Peery, A. (2021). *PLC-Powered Data Teams: A Guide to Effective Collaboration and Learning*. Rexford, NY: International Center for Leadership in Education.

Peery, A., Patrick, P., & Moore, D. (2013). *Ask Don't Tell: Powerful Questioning in the Classroom*. Englewood, CO: Lead + Learn Press.

Pendharkar, E. (2021, June 17). More Than 1 Million Students Didn't Enroll During the Pandemic. Will They Come Back? *Education Week*. https://www.edweek.org/leadership/more-than-1-million-students-didnt-enroll-during-the-pandemic-will-they-come-back/2021/06

Quaglia, R., Fox, K., Lande, L., & Young, D. (2020). The Power of Voice in Schools: Listening, Learning, and Leading Together. *ASCD*.

Reeves, D. (2021). *Fearless Schools: Building Trust and Resilience for Learning, Teaching, and Leading*. Boston, MA: Creative Leadership Press.

Reeves, D. (2020). *Achieving Equity and Excellence: Immediate Results from the Lessons of High-Poverty, High-Success Schools*. Bloomington, IN: Solution Tree Press.

Reeves, D., & DuFour, R. (2016, March 1). The Futility of PLC Lite. *Phi Delta Kappan*, *97*(6), 69–71. https://kappanonline.org/the-futility-of-plc-lite/

Rhew, E., Piro, J. S., Goolkasian, P., & Cosentino, P. (2018). The Effects of a Growth Mindset on Self-Efficacy and Motivation. *Cogent Education*, *5*(1), 1492337. https://doi.org/10.1080/2331186X.2018.1492337

Rita Pierson: Every Kid Needs a Champion | TED. (2013). https://www.youtube.com/watch?v=SFnMTHhKdkw

Roderick, M. (1994). Grade Retention and School Dropout: Investigating the Association. *American Educational Research Journal*, *31*(4), 729–759. http://www.jstor.org/stable/1163393

Roderick, M., & Camburn, E. (1999). Risk and Recovery from Course Failure in the Early Years of High School. *American Educational Research Journal*, *36*(2), 303–343. https://doi.org/10.2307/1163541

Roderick, M., & Nagaoka, J. (2005). Retention under Chicago's High-Stakes Testing Program: Helpful, Harmful, or Harmless? *Educational Evaluation and Policy Analysis*, *27*(4), 309–340. http://www.jstor.org/stable/3699564

Rodriguez, E. R., & Bellanca, J. (2017). *What is it About Me You Can't Teach: Culturally Responsive Instruction in Deeper Learning Classrooms* (3rd ed.). Thousand Oaks, CA: Corwin Press.

Roller, T. [@DegaSuper]. (2018, July 22). One never knows what that student in the back of the room suffering from the 4 downs will grow up to be! Head down wearing hand me downs and a downtrodden outlook on life [Twitter]. Twitter. https://twitter.com/DegaSuper/status/1021255044841328643

Ryzin, M. J. V. (2021). *Small-Group Learning Can Mitigate the Effects of School Closures – but Only if Teachers Use It Well*. The Conversation. http://theconversation.com/small-group-learning-can-mitigate-the-effects-of-school-closures-but-only-if-teachers-use-it-well-170701

Scanfeld, V., Davis, L., Weintraub, L., & Dotoli, V. (2018, September 1). The Power of Common Language. ASCD. https://www.ascd.org/el/articles/the-power-of-common-language

Schlechty, P. C. (2011). *Engaging Students: The Next Level of Working on the Work*. San Francisco, CA: Jossey Bass.

Sethi, J., & Scales, P. C. (2020). Developmental Relationships and School Success: How Teachers, Parents, and Friends Affect Educational

Outcomes and What Actions Students Say Matter Most. *Contemporary Educational Psychology*, *63*, 101904. https://doi.org/10.1016/j.cedpsych.2020.101904

Smith, Z. S. (2022, March 31). More High Schoolers Felt Hopeless Or Suicidal During Pandemic As Mental Health Crisis Intensified, CDC Finds. *Forbes*. https://www.forbes.com/sites/zacharysmith/2022/03/31/more-high-schoolers-felt-hopeless-or-suicidal-during-pandemic-as-mental-health-crisis-intensified-cdc-finds/

Sousa, D. A. (2015). *Engaging the Rewired Brain* (1st ed.). West Palm Beach, FL: Learning Sciences International.

Sparks, S. D. (2015, November 7). Study: RTI Practice Falls Short of Promise. *Education Week*. https://www.edweek.org/teaching-learning/study-rti-practice-falls-short-of-promise/2015/11

State Education Practices (SEP). (2017). https://nces.ed.gov/programs/statereform/tab5_1.asp

Students Weigh In, Part III: Learning & Well-Being During COVID-19. (2021). *YouthTruth*. https://youthtruthsurvey.org/students-weigh-in-part3/

Tackie, H. N. (2022). (Dis)Connected: Establishing Social Presence and Intimacy in Teacher–Student Relationships During Emergency Remote Learning. *AERA Open*, *8*, 233285842110695. https://doi.org/10.1177/23328584211069525

The Power of Relationships in Schools. (2019, January 14). https://www.edutopia.org/video/power-relationships-schools

Toth, M. D. (2021). *Why Student Engagement Is Important in a Post-COVID World*. Learning Sciences International. https://www.learningsciences.com/blog/why-is-student-engagement-important/

Trust, E., & MDRC. (2021). The Importance of Strong Relationships - A Strategy to Solve Unfinished Learning. *The Education Trust*. https://edtrust.org/resource/the-importance-of-strong-relationships/

Vaish, V. (2013). Questioning and Oracy in a Reading Program. *Language and Education*, *27*(6), 526–541. https://doi.org/10.1080/09500782.2012.737334

Van Marter Souers, K., & Hall, P. (2020, October 1). Trauma Is a Word—Not a Sentence. *ASCD*. https://www.ascd.org/el/articles/trauma-is-a-word-not-a-sentence?_hsenc=p2ANqtz-8DPASI-JoUsddLms3h-NoBww2xm0yehN_R1WWreqmMsYZ60EjD098Bs7uV0xwV18Ny-5SUwnur-FH4H203sAodJEQixa_g&_hsmi=97067975

Venables, D. (2019, July 1). *So, How Are We Going to Teach This?* ASCD. https://www.ascd.org/el/articles/so-how-are-we-going-to-teach-this

Visible Learning Meta^X ™ -Home (2021). https://www.visiblelearning-metax.com/Influences

Vogler, K. (2008, June 1). *Asking Good Questions*. ASCD. https://www.ascd.org/el/articles/asking-good-questions

Walker, T. (2021, November 29). *Why Pronouncing Students' Names Correctly is So Important | NEA*. https://www.nea.org/advocating-for-change/new-from-nea/why-pronouncing-students-names-correctly-so-important

Walsh, J. A., & Sattes, B. D. (2015, September). A New Rhythm for Responding. *ASCD*. https://www.ascd.org/el/articles/a-new-rhythm-for-responding

Watson, J., & Gemin, B. (2008). *Promising Practices in Online Learning: Using Online Learning for At-Risk Students and Credit Recovery*. Vienna, VA: North American Council for Online Learning. http://www.nacol.org/promisingpractices/NACOL_CreditRecovery_Promising-Practices.pdf

Wehlage, G. G., & Rutter, R. A. (1985). Dropping Out: How Much Do Schools Contribute to the Problem? *Wisconsin Center for Education Research*. Retrieved from http://www.eric.ed.gov/PDFS/ED275799.pdf

What is the QFT? (n.d.). Right Question Institute. Retrieved May 24, 2022, from https://rightquestion.org/what-is-the-qft/

Willis, J. (2014, July 18). The Neuroscience behind Stress and Learning. *Edutopia*. https://www.edutopia.org/blog/neuroscience-behind-stress-and-learning-judy-willis

Wlodkowski, R. J. (1983). *Motivational Opportunities for Successful Teaching* [Leader's Guide]. Phoenix, AZ: Universal Dimensions.

Wong, H., Wong, R., Rogers, K., & Brooks, A. (2012). Managing Your Classroom for Success. *Science and Children, 49*(9), 60–64. http://www.jstor.org/stable/43747385

Wormeli, R. (2011, November 1). Redos and Retakes Done Right. *ASCD*. https://www.ascd.org/el/articles/redos-and-retakes-done-right

Wright, A. (2021). *Pandemic Prompts Some States to Pass Struggling Third Graders. Stateline*, an initiative of The Pew Charitable Trusts. https://pew.org/2SaPafJ

Zakrzewski, V. (2012, November 6). How to Help Students Develop Hope. *Greater Good*. https://greatergood.berkeley.edu/article/item/how_to_help_students_develop_hope

Zwiers, J., & Crawford, M. (2011). *Academic Conversations: Classroom Talk That Fosters Critical Thinking and Content Understandings*. Portland, ME: Stenhouse Publishers.

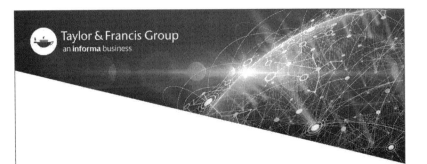

Made in the USA
Middletown, DE
22 February 2023

25415006R00066